Routledge Revivals

Malaya and its History

First published in 1948, *Malaya and its History* is a history of Malaya ranging from the thousand years of Hindu influence to the eras of Portuguese and Dutch rule, and from the establishment of the British protectorate to Malayan independence in 1957. There are chapters on law, trade, industry and the social services. This book will be of interest to students of history, southeast Asian studies, and cultural studies.

Malay and its History

R. O. Winstedt

Routledge
Taylor & Francis Group

First published in July 1948
Second edition February 1951
Third edition November 1953
Fourth edition May 1956
Fifth edition April 1958
Sixth edition April 1962
Seventh edition March 1966
By Hutchinson & Co (Publishers) Ltd.

This edition first published in 2024 by Routledge
4 Park Square, Milton Park, Abingdon, Oxon, OX14 4RN

and by Routledge
605 Third Avenue, New York, NY 10017

Routledge is an imprint of the Taylor & Francis Group, an informa business

© for new material Richard Winstedt 1962 and 1966

All rights reserved. No part of this book may be reprinted or reproduced or utilised in any form or by any electronic, mechanical, or other means, now known or hereafter invented, including photocopying and recording, or in any information storage or retrieval system, without permission in writing from the publishers.

Publisher's Note
The publisher has gone to great lengths to ensure the quality of this reprint but points out that some imperfections in the original copies may be apparent.

Disclaimer
The publisher has made every effort to trace copyright holders and welcomes correspondence from those they have been unable to contact.

A Library of Congress record exists under LCCN: 66071804

ISBN: 978-1-032-73497-2 (hbk)
ISBN: 978-1-003-46449-5 (ebk)
ISBN: 978-1-032-73498-9 (pbk)

Book DOI 10.4324/9781003464495

MALAYA
AND ITS HISTORY

Sir Richard Winstedt
KBE, CMG, FBA, D.LITT (OXON), MA
HON. LL.D (MALAYA)

formerly of the Malayan Civil Service
and Reader in Malay in the University of London

HUTCHINSON UNIVERSITY LIBRARY
LONDON

HUTCHINSON & CO (*Publishers*) LTD
178–202 Great Portland Street, London W1

London Melbourne Sydney
Auckland Bombay Toronto
Johannesburg New York

First published July 1948
Second Edition February 1951
Third Edition November 1953
Fourth Edition May 1956
Reprinted May 1957
Fifth Edition April 1958
Sixth Edition April 1962
Seventh Edition March 1966

The paperback edition of this book is sold subject to the condition that it shall not, by way of trade, be lent, re-sold, hired out or otherwise disposed of without the publisher's consent, in any form of binding or cover other than that in which it is published

© for new material Richard Winstedt 1962 and 1966

This book has been set in Imprint, printed in Great Britain on Smooth Wove paper by Anchor Press, and bound by Wm. Brendon, both of Tiptree, Essex

CONTENTS

I	Malaya—the land	7
II	The peoples	13
III	The Hindu millennium	24
IV	Malacca's century of Malay rule	32
V	A Famosa	40
VI	The Dutch at Malacca	47
VII	The Straits settlements	53
VIII	Britain and the Malay states	62
IX	British administration	78
X	The reign of law	96
XI	Trade, monopolized and free, and finance	103
XII	Industries, past and present	112
XIII	Labour: health: education	124
XIV	Japan's hour of triumph	135
XV	The Malayan union and Singapore	140
XVI	An independent Malaya and a self-governing Singapore	148
	Bibliography	155
	Index	161

CHAPTER I

MALAYA—THE LAND

i

SEVEN times the Malay Peninsula has played a notable part on the world's stage. About 6000 B.C. it was a bridge down which the ancestors of the Australian aborigine and of the Papuan made their way to the narrow waters they crossed one after another to their present homes. About 2000 B.C. the ancestors of the Malays descended its rivers on their trek from Yunnan to Sumatra and Java and beyond. Then, when India and China had built ships for the high seas, a Malay Buddhist empire, Sri Vijaya, maintained a footing in the north of the peninsula to command the Straits of Malacca, as it maintained a footing in Palembang to command the Sunda Straits. For five centuries the fleets of its Maharaja intercepted ships faring between India and China to levy tribute and toll, as afterwards the fleets of Portuguese and Dutch monopolists were to do. In the fourteenth century Sri Vijaya and its colonies fell before the attacks of Majapahit, Java's last Hindu empire, and one of its fugitive princes founded about 1403 the port kingdom of Malacca to be for a hundred years a Malay world market. In addition (a happening even more momentous) Malacca became a centre from which Indian and Arab missionaries carried the religion of Muhammad to the islands of the archipelago.

Then came the European. In 1511 d'Albuquerque captured Malacca to be Portugal's base for trade with the Spice Islands and the Far East. From Portugal it was wrested in 1641 by the Dutch, who, having settled at Batavia to command the Sunda Straits, wanted, like Sri Vijaya, to dominate the Straits of Malacca also, the more effectively to hold the East and West in fee. Under Dutch rule Malacca, after nearly two and a half centuries of greatness, was eclipsed by Batavia, and when in the nineteenth century it was transferred to Great Britain, the increased draught of East Indiamen had already made it a less convenient port of call than Raffles' "political child" Singapore, where the introduction of free trade furnished modern Asia with a new pattern of commerce and government. A century later the demand of the motor industry for tin and rubber lifted Singapore into one of the world's ten greatest ports. In 1941 the capture of that key to the Pacific by the Japanese saw the defence of Netherlands India collapse like a house of cards, and exposed India and Australia to menace.

So much we know of Malaya's past and more, although Muslim fanaticism destroyed nearly all the vestiges of its Hindu period and British engineers blasted the fourteenth-century monument to Majapahit's conquest of Singapore, blew up Malacca's mediaeval Portuguese fortress and used the bricks of a Dutch fort in Lower Perak to make roads.

Wave after wave of early migrants visited the Malay peninsula and aborigines stayed behind on its mountains, although it was not till the Christian era that states emerged into history, already called after rivers with Malay names or bearing Sanskrit names introduced by sparse Indian colonists. For the whole peninsula there was until the nineteenth century no common label, rivers giving their separate names to those sections of the limitless forest into which they cut the only openings. By Malays it came to be termed "Malay land" (*tanah Mĕlayu*), though parts of Sumatra and Borneo are also "Malay land". The continent of Europe still calls the country the Peninsula of Malacca. But it was the British whose roads first pierced the great forest and joined river states, and it was left for the British to employ a suitable name for the whole peninsula. When and by whom was that name, Malaya, invented? It occurs in *Mendez Pinto* (1539), in Leyden's *Dirge of the Departed Year*, written in 1806, and again in Captain Sherard Osborn's pleasant book on *Quedah*, which was published in London in 1857 but written as a diary when he was a midshipman in Malayan waters.

It was, however, not till the present century that the name became popular. British Malaya it was sometimes amplified, to distinguish between British and Siamese Malaya. But as their

MALAYA—THE LAND 9

states were protectorates and not colonies, Malays resented the adjective, bitterly after a Union was mooted. And apart from the euphonious Malaya, the peninsula was singularly unfortunate in names of British invention: Prince of Wales' Island for a settlement never called by any name but Penang; Straits Settlements, an unromantic description for the Colony, with a penal nuance; Malayan Union, a term reminiscent of poor-houses and primers on political science. "Malaya" the peninsula is called by all races, and, happily when independent, Malaya it remains. Malaya fits the new country of tin and rubber, but it fits also the country of Swettenham's *Real Malay* and Hugh Clifford's *Brown Humanity* and George Maxwell's *In Malay Forests*, the country of palm and mangrove and tawny rivers.

ii

That part of Malaya which fell within the British sphere was a little larger than England without Wales. Hardly a quarter of the area has been hacked out of the sea of forest. The species of trees exceed in number all those of India and Burma, and flowering plants and ferns amount to more than 9000.

There are three kinds of forest. Above 2000 feet is one of low trees, lichens, mosses, ferns, liverworts and orchids. Below that height is another type with the vegetation most characteristic of the country, ranging from trees 150 to 200 feet tall down to a dense undergrowth of palms, tree-ferns and herbaceous plants. Along the coast the forest changes again. Wherever there are sandy spits or rocky soil, the graceful casuarina flourishes, and wherever there are mud-flats, mile upon mile of mangrove trees straddle the ooze.

Mountains and rivers are big for the size of the country. The highest mountain, Gunong Tahan, which lies on the northern frontier of Pahang, rises to 7184 feet, and the next highest (7160 feet) is one of the granite peaks of the main range, named by the Indonesian Sakai Korbu, meaning "Mountain"

—though modern Malays and map-makers have corrupted it into Kerbau—"Buffalo". For, excepting a large area of freshwater swamps, each type of soil covered by the different kinds of forest has supported different races. Like their kinsmen the Igorots of Luzon and the Bataks of Sumatra, the Sakai have felled clearings on mountain slopes, and the higher the sites, the healthier and more intelligent the tribe. On the level land the Malays are to be found: attracted by the rice-plains of the north, and, since commerce visited their shores, by the jungle produce, resin, guttapercha, rattans, and by tin and gold, they used for their highways the rivers, the Kelantan, the Trengganu, the Pahang, the Johore, the Selangor, the Perak, the Kedah, all of which have given their names to Malay states. Finally, along the coastal belt and at the estuaries settled the Malay sea-gipsies, fishermen and, with the coming of Indian commerce, pirates, whose ancestors, for example, formed an element in the population of Sri Vijaya and of mediaeval Malacca.

But country broken into small valleys afforded little promise of livelihood for an agricultural people in days before international commerce opened markets for metals and jungle produce. When they descended from the continent of Asia, Malays had already learnt to irrigate rice-fields; so at the wide plains of northern Malaya, Perlis, Kedah and Kelantan, a wave of Malay agriculturists halted. There in the north a large Malay population collected, leaving the more southerly part of the peninsula to nomad aborigines and Malay sea-gipsies until in mediaeval times it, too, was developed by the aforesaid sea-tribes, by Minangkabaus who colonized Negri Sembilan and by Bugis who colonized Selangor.

Like every tropical country, Malaya is always green and always beautiful, though not perhaps as beautiful as Ceylon or Java or as varied in its landscape as Indo-China. But, except in valleys where rice-fields have been cut out of the jungle, as, for example, in Kedah, Perlis and Kelantan, in Malacca and Negri Sembilan, it is only from some mountain height that the visitor can get free of the enclosing forest and rubber estates and confront landscape in perspective.

Few nowadays get the chance to travel by Malayan rivers,

past avenues of trees of all shades, hung with veils of smoky-grey or orange-flowered creepers, past clumps of feathery bamboo and white-leaved bushes and plants with crimson tassels or rosemadder fringes. Fewer still know the fairy beauty of the islands off the east coast or of the Langkawis that from the Peak at Penang can be descried far off in a setting of cloud-chased peacock sea. Across the harbour of Penang towers Kedah Peak, purple at sunrise above the willow-green shoots or golden grain of rice-fields. Penang, beyond dispute, is one of the world's fairest spots.

Seldom in a sea of forest does the wayfarer light on elephant or tiger or rhinoceros or the wild bison or deer or many of the 650 species of birds. In the jungle of Pahang and Johore is a huge bearded pig, but even hunters have encountered them so seldom that it was a moot point whether they had not been imported in the last 50 years, until at last their skeletal remains were unearthed among the prehistoric litter of a Kelantan cave. Crocodiles one may see in every river, nor are iguanas or monkeys shy. Once in a lifetime, if the fates are kind, the traveller may catch a glimpse of a pack of the red fox-like wild dogs in hot chase across a clearing, or surprise a baby tapir at his bath. There are over 130 varieties of snakes, and some 800 butterflies and 200 dragon-flies. The fauna of the mountains is closely related to that of the Himalayan ranges, but, curiously enough, there are affinities between the birds and insects of Malaya and West Africa.

It is a pity that Malaya was a *terra incognita* to the Victorian lady who wrote to a friend in 1841, "When I say romantic, I mean damp." On 27 December, 1926, there fell at Kemaman in Trengganu 15½ inches of rain, and Trengganu's total rainfall for the month was 76.54 inches. In the same month the Perak River rose 38½ feet at Kuala Kangsar and the Pahang River over 60 feet at Temerloh. That year was abnormal. Ordinarily the annual rainfall varies between 50 inches in the driest locality and 259 inches in the mountains. During December and January the east coast of Malaya is swept by the north-east monsoon blowing across the China Sea. From May to October, tempered by Sumatra's mountains, the south-west monsoon prevails. To get an idea of the temperature it is only necessary to visit the palm-house at Kew. In the hottest spot on the plains the mean daily maximum is about 95°F. in the shade; on the highest mountains night has seen it fall to less than half that. The early mornings are delightful and the nights tolerable.

CHAPTER II

THE PEOPLES

ABORIGINES

THE most primitive race extant in south-east Asia and the Malay archipelago is that of the dwarf Negritos, called Semang in Kedah and Perak, and Pangan in Kelantan. These little black woolly-headed nomads are related to the Aetas of the Philippines and the Mincopies of the Andaman Islands. In Malaya there are some thousands of them, living on jungle fruits, roots and game. Their weapon is the bow and arrow, but they have borrowed the blow-pipe of the Sakai, with whom they have intermarried. They build neither houses nor boats, but sleep round a forest fire on a floor of sticks under a wall-less leaf shelter propped on a stick. Innocent of the crimes that spring from greed and passion, they live in family groups with no ruling class or tribal organization. They fear thunder and lightning and draw blood from their shins to appease the unseen powers that cause them.

Far higher in the scale of civilization are the taller, fair, wavy-haired Sakai or Senoi of the mountains and foot-hills. They are cinnamon-coloured people of Indonesian stock, which is one of the components of the Malay race, but their language is mainly Mon-Annam. They are akin to hill-tribes in Yunnan, Indo-China and the Malay archipelago, but those of the lower hills have not only intermarried with the Negrito in the north and the Jakun or proto-Malay in the south but exhibit an Australo-Melanesoid strain; that is, traces of the blood of the remote ancestors of the Papuans and of Australia's aborigines. There are some 24,000 Sakai, divided into tribes and families under patriarchal chiefs. Their houses, like those of the Malays, are built on piles, and they plant rice, sugar, millet, plantain and tobacco, moving to fresh clearings as the soil becomes exhausted. Like the primitive Malay, they are animists, fearing innumerable spirits of sickness. Like the Malay and the Mongol, they believe in the shaman, giving him as the Malay once did tree-burial, to let the tiger familiar rend his body and release his spirit.

In the southern half of British Malaya are found primitive tribes, whose proto-Malay ancestors trekked down from Yunnan and overran Indo-China. Whether of the land or sea these Jakun, as they call themselves, have the Indonesian and Mongoloid strains that, along with foreign blood acquired in historical times, make up the modern civilized Malay. But some of them also exhibit the very early Australo-Melanesoid blood and one may see a Johore Jakun as big, black and bearded as a Papuan. The jungle tribes live on fruits and wild game and the Orang Laut (Kipling's "Orange Lord") or Sea-Folk by fishing, their families with them in their boats or ashore in huts. These sea-tribes would transfix fish with wooden spears, and in modern times they dive for coins in Singapore dock. Tomé Pires, the Portuguese writer (1515), was the first to term them "Cellates", which may mean People of the *Sĕlat* or Straits. He describes them as pirates who haunted the Carimon (*Kĕrimun*) islands, showed the port of Malacca to its founder and took part with their blow-pipes in its defence against d'Albuquerque. He adds that the founder of Malacca rewarded these aboriginal followers by bestowing on them titles and offices such as that of Bendahara or Prime Minister and Laksamana or Admiral, which would make them the ancestors of leading Malay families. In the eighteenth century they were still loyal followers of the sultans of Johore, who condescendingly bestowed on them grandiloquent titles. Their religion is animism, the belief that stocks and stones are animated by living spirits, but from their civilized neighbours they learnt also to invoke Hindu deities. Their language is Malay, free from foreign loan-words.

More and more Malaya's aborigines are ceasing to be nomadic.

The Civilized Malay

The migration of the Malays from Yunnan down to the Malay peninsula took place between 2500 and 1500 B.C. Their quadrangular adze culture, accompanied by unglazed cord-marked pottery of great variety, has been traced from China southward, and "the highly specialized pick-adzes of Java and Sumatra from a simple adze type with quadrangular cross-section and semi-circular edge found in Laos through an intermediate type frequent in Malaya indicates the direction and way of their migration"—namely, down the Malay peninsula. Some may have travelled by land, others across the Gulf of Siam in craft developed from bamboo outriggers still in use on rivers in Burma and Indo-China. Among the earliest waves may have been the Jakun. But the most important movement brought the ancestors of the Malays of Kedah, Kelantan and Patani to become the civilized hinduized subjects of Langkasuka and Sri Vijaya. The people of Kelantan, who have been compared to the Polynesians, are bigger than the Malays of the south, perhaps because they represent a different strain, perhaps on account of a better climate or the better food of an ancient rice and fishing area.

For the culture of primitive Malays, language and prehistoric discoveries provide the only evidence. And while earlier peoples, apparently with an Australo-Melanesoid strain, lived in caves or left gigantic shell-heaps, the debris of antediluvian meals, to bear witness to their location, the more highly civilized Indonesian and primitive Malay inhabited villages that are revealed only by some accident like the great flood of 1926, which unearthed one at Tembeling in Pahang. Yet there is ample evidence that, before these neolithic people left the continent of Asia, they made pottery and built megaliths. They were hunters—not only of game but of human heads for the sake of their soul-substance. They were fishermen acquainted with traps of bamboo and wood, though not, apparently, with the cast-net or other nets of cord. They lived, as villagers still live, in houses built on piles and lashed with rattan, with bamboo flooring and walls. In their gardens they cultivated sugarcane, bananas, the gourd and the coconut. Their field-crops were millet (still a Sakai crop) and rice, both of which provided them with food and fermented drink. They had domesticated the pig and the buffalo and perhaps cattle. Their clothes were of bark. Their numerals went up to a thousand and they possessed some knowledge of the stars.

It must have been long before the Christian era that Malay names were given to many parts of Malaya like Kelantan, Muar and Tumasik (which Hindus changed to Singapore). The meaning of Naning, for example, is forgotten today, but we know from the Malay element in the Khasi of Assam that it means "Upriver". Possibly no generic name was adopted by the scattered tribes until Jambi or Melayu succeeded Sri Vijaya in the thirteenth century, after which they called themselves Malays.

When Jambi fell, Minangkabau dominated Sumatra. And when Malacca was founded with a population largely made up of Malay sea-gipsies, its commerce attracted many Malays from the opposite coast of Sumatra, more especially Hindu Minangkabaus, who sought the gold districts of Pahang and the valleys of what in the eighteenth century became Negri Sembilan. Bugis, too, from Celebes, in 1700 founded modern Selangor and in 1722 became Underkings of the Johore empire. Most of the Bugis immigrants, at any rate, were men of birth who intermarried with peninsular royalties and dominated their local Malay subjects. Yet to infer from the legends of the *Malay Annals* that most of the Malays of the peninsula crossed from Sumatra in mediaeval times is to ignore the evidence of prehistory and place-names. The Malays have at least as much right to be regarded as the aboriginal people of Malaya as the English have to be called the aborigines of England.

The Malay of today, a broad-headed individual with olive skin, fine eyes, a neat well-proportioned body, lank black hair and almost hairless chin, is the primitive Malay plus many foreign strains derived from marriage with Chinese from Chou times down to the advent of Islam, with Hindus of the Deccan and Bengal, with Muslim Indians, Siamese and Arabs. They have changed little since Magellan's brother-in-law, Duarte Barbosa, described them from his experience in the East between 1500 and 1517: "They are well-set-up men and go bare from the waist up but are clad in cotton garments below. They, the most distinguished among them, wear short coats which come half-way down their thighs, of silk cloth—in grain or brocade—and over this they wear girdles; at their waists they carry daggers in damascene-work which they call creeses.

Their women are tawny-coloured, clad in very fine silk garments and short skirts decorated with gold and jewels. They are very comely, always well-attired and have very fine hair. . . . They live in large houses outside the city with many orchards, gardens and tanks, where they lead a pleasant life. They are polished and well-bred, fond of music and given to love."

To bring the picture up to date: all but the peasant at work in his fields wear coats nowadays, creeses are worn only at court ceremonies, and many Malays have adopted European dress for working hours. When a British Resident once issued a circular in praise of Malay costume and in favour of its retention, the Malay chiefs at the next meeting of the State Council asked him the reason: was he concerned lest they should contract dhobi[1]-itch?

It is a pity that modern life and the Malay's own admiration for European ways have conspired to make the white man forget what Miss Isabella Bird, author of *The Golden Chersonese*, knew in 1879: "The Malays undoubtedly must be numbered among civilized peoples. . . . They have possessed for centuries systems of government and codes of land and maritime law, which in theory at least show a considerable degree of enlightenment."

The Malay has great pride of race—due, perhaps, as much to his Islamic religion as to a past he has forgotten. He has, as Sir Frank Swettenham once wrote, "as good a courage as most men", and a better sense of the values of what life offers than is generally gained from book philosophies. Even the aborigines of Malaya have attractive manners, and the Malay has not only undergone the discipline of Hindu etiquette but has been affected by his Muslim teaching much as an English boy has been affected by the public school, acquiring poise and confidence. Because he is an independent farmer with no need to work for hire, the Malay has got an undeserved reputation for idleness, which his Asiatic competitors take care to foster. In affairs he is not only diplomatic but intelligent and statesmanlike, with a natural ability to weigh both sides of a question. His domestic life is happy. He marries young, but in spite of the latitude of Islamic practice the peasant has seldom been a

[1] Hindustani for "laundryman".

polygamist, though the immemorial need for sons to work his fields makes him prone to repudiate a childless wife.

At the 1947 census, out of 2,398,186 Malays in the Federation, 275,700 were comparatively new-comers from Sumatra and Java, men of the Malay's own racial stock and religion, who alone of the country's immigrants rapidly become absorbed into the Malay community. In the Federation the 1957 census showed 3,126,706 Malays, 2,332,936 Chinese, 695,985 Indians and Pakistanis, and 123,136 persons of other races. In Kelantan the population is almost wholly Malay.

CHINESE

Chinese may have visited Malaya in pre-historic times. The first historical record, the Chinese *History of the Leang* (502–556), mentions Langkasuka, a Buddhist state in the north of Malaya whose rulers sent embassies to China at least four times during the sixth century A.D. What part the Chinese played in the peninsular half of Sri Vijaya is unknown. But when at the end of the fourteenth century that empire fell, the Chinese established at Palembang in Sri Vijaya's Sumatran centre "stood up for themselves and a man from Namhoi in Canton, called Liang Tan-ming, who had lived there a long time and roamed the sea, followed by several thousand men from Fukien and Canton, was taken by them as their chief". For nearly 200 years Palembang remained in the hands of Chinese, who were, many of them, pirates.

The first Malay mention of Chinese in the peninsula is found in the *Malay Annals* of fifteenth-century Malacca. Mixing folklore and history, they relate how the Emperor sent Sultan Mansur Shah (*ca.* 1456) a junk full of needles as many as the people of China, and how the Malay king sent back envoys with a cargo of sago, every bead rolled by one of his subjects. The Malays entered the seven gates of the imperial palace to the clash of gongs and saw the Emperor in a glass palanquin carried in the mouth of a dragon. They brought back for the Sultan a "royal" bride, Hang Liu, whose escort of 500 gentry settled in Malacca and gave Bukit China its name.

Tomé Pires, the Portuguese who lived in Malacca from 1512 to 1515, is less romantic. "The Chinese to be seen in Malacca are not very truthful and steal. That is the common people." But Tomé Pires says that Islam had not yet got a strong enough hold over the Malays to prevent intermarriage with the Chinese. "Heathens marry with Moorish" (that is, Muslim) "women and a Moor with a heathen woman with their own proper ceremonies." Afterwards, when Malays became strict Muslims, the Chinese immigrants forbidden to bring their wives from China had to turn to Balinese and Batak slaves to be the mothers of a Baba race, which by intermarriage among its own kith and kin retained Chinese dress and Chinese customs though it lost Chinese speech. Under the Dutch there were about 2000 Babas in eighteenth-century Malacca, some employed as soldiers. A Perak history, written in the same century, relates how Chinese boxers and snake-charmers took part in royal festivities there with Chinese music that sounded "like the noise of frogs in a swamp after rain".

The Chinese words in the Babas' pidgin Malay support the claim of the Hokkiens from Amoy that they were the earliest immigrants and they are still more numerous than other Chinese in the former Straits Settlements and Johore. But it was Western trade after the Napoleonic wars and then tin and finally rubber that attracted an endless flow of Chinese from Kwangtung (Canton) as well as from Fukien to Penang, Singapore and the Malay States as they came under British rule. The stream has also included Khehs (or Hakkas), Teochus, many of whom are fishermen, and the so-called Hailams from the island of Hainan who are excellent and well-bred domestic servants and shop-keepers and small planters.

Nearly all the commerce of Malaya is in Chinese hands. There are Chinese planters, miners, bankers, doctors, lawyers, accountants, civil servants, schoolmasters, contractors, rubber manufacturers, timber merchants, booksellers, hotel-keepers, pig-rearers, poultry-farmers, market-gardeners, carpenters and fishermen. Without the Chinese, Malaya, having no surplus population of unemployed Malays, could never have developed. But Chinese national virtues are colonial vices. Against a people so industrious, intelligent and clannish, no other race can stand up. Endowed with the laughter and manners of an ancient civilization, they mix with other races with innate good nature and are delighted to welcome them to their entertainments, but never into their businesses. No trespasser may ever enter their commercial preserves. In colonial politics they have been even less interested than in Chinese politics, a trait that has made their invasion into local commerce less patent. Never till the British period did they attempt to take part in the administration of Malaya.

In 1947 two-thirds of the Chinese in Malaya were born in their own country and were remitting their savings to their native districts, thereby draining Malaya of a great portion of its wealth. Now that more and more Chinese are born in Malaya, this drain on the country's wealth will lessen, but racial competition will be aggravated. In 1957 there were 1,141,800 Chinese in Singapore and 207,300 Malaysians: the figures for the Federation have been given above (p. 18).

INDIANS

For more than a thousand years the Malays owed their civilization to Hindus, though the Indian immigrants, whether from the Deccan or Bengal, were never enough to introduce their own colloquial languages and had to be content to introduce Indian alphabets, the last the Perso-Arabic Muslim alphabet that has been known to the Malays for 600 years. The coming of Islam to India stimulated Indian migration to the peninsula. According to Tomé Pires, when Diogo Lopes de Sequeira reached Malacca there were a thousand Gujerati merchants there, or, along with Parsis, Bengalis and Arabs, more than 4000 foreigners. "There were also great Kling merchants with trade on a great scale and many junks. This is the nation that brings most honour to Malacca." By local usage all southern Indians, Tamils, Telugus and Malayalis are called Klings after the mediaeval kingdom of Kalinga that covered the northern Circars or territory north of the Coromandel coast, but though the use of the term is a tribute to the greatness of his past, the southern Indian now regards it as derogatory. The Malay, for his part, has borrowed the word "Lebai" as a term of respect for a pious Malay elder from the Labbai Muslims of the Madras coast. Tamil merchants occasionally won place and honour in old Malacca and in eighteenth-century Perak, where the Sultan gave one a title for going to India and returning with a trader who bought elephants. Half-caste Indians, like Munshi 'Abdullah, who was half Tamil and half Arab, have played a great part in writing the Malay's literature of translation, introducing him to Indian folk-lore, romance and mysticism. Today the great majority of Indians in Malaya are Tamil labourers from the Madras Presidency, who work on rubber estates, on the railway and in the Public Works Department and return home on an average after three years. Most Tamils of the second generation are clerks, overseers and schoolmasters. Malaya also has Indian doctors, lawyers and merchants.

Northern Indians are fewer, but include men of many races: Punjabis, Bengalis, Afghans, Pathans and Mahrattas. Many Punjabi Sikhs and a few Pathans are policemen. From Ceylon come not only Tamil clerks but a few thousand Singhalese jewellers, carpenters, barbers and labourers. In 1955 there were just under 775,485 Indians, Pakistanis and Ceylonese in Malaya, of whom 695,985 were in the Federation.

OTHER RACES

The northern states, having been subject to Siam until 1909, have a large sprinkling of Siamese residents.

Arabs, though only a few thousand in number, have great influence from their religious status and their wealth. In Singapore, nearly all the Arabs are of pure Arab descent, most of them immigrants from the Hadramaut, where they have built palatial houses with fittings imported from Singapore. The war, it may be noted, greatly impoverished the Hadramaut by depriving its people of the usual remittances from Malaya and Netherlands India. As early as the seventeenth century Sayids (or descendants of the Prophet) of the great Hadramaut house of Ahmad Isa al-Mohajir had won State offices in Perak. One became the father of a Perak Sultan. From another are descended the rulers of Siak in Sumatra. The older settlers have intermarried with Malay women. But a Sharifah, the female equivalent of a Sayid, may marry no one but a Sayid or a Malay of raja rank.

In 1947 there were about a thousand Jews, some of them the wealthy owners of large properties in Singapore.

Filipinos, Boyanese, Bataks, Tibetans, Annamese, Negro boxers, Turks and many local races add to Malaya's human miscellany. But the only two races numerous enough to require mention are Eurasians and Europeans, who in 1947 numbered respectively 19,171 and 18,958, almost equally distributed between Singapore and the Federation.

Malaya's Eurasians of oldest descent are those with Portuguese blood in their veins and a *patois* founded on mediaeval Portuguese. All of them came originally from Malacca, where the poorest are fishermen and the well-to-do planters, clerks and schoolmasters. All Portuguese Eurasians are Catholics. But there are also several well-known Eurasian families in Malaya who are of Dutch descent and again derive from Malacca. The prosperity of Penang and Singapore later attracted Eurasians from British India, some descendants of writers and captains in the East India Company. A son of Captain Light, the founder of Penang, by a Portuguese Eurasian was an officer on Wellington's staff and laid out Adelaide. The Eurasians of Malaya refused to follow the example of Eurasians in India, who term themselves Anglo-Indians. They have to their credit such a record of respectability and public service that it would have been a pity for them to disguise their identity.

Lastly there are the Europeans of whom in 1947 there were in the Federation only 9986. They numbered representatives of most European countries and of the United States of America. All the British are employed in business, planting or mining, or they are private doctors, lawyers, accountants or journalists, and a few temporarily at least are government servants. Europeans and Eurasians are now classed as "other races" in government reports. While there were no localities confined to Europeans, in larger towns they have had their own clubs, just as Chinese, Malays, Indians and Eurasians have theirs. Superficial observers believe the Asian is eager to enter European clubs. But he would be no happier if all clubs were mixed than the European would be. Generally he prefers to associate with his own race. And had the Eurasians or the British, for example, admitted Chinese to membership of their clubs, they would have been entirely swamped by the more numerous community. But there are more and more clubs with an international membership, one of the most successful of them founded by Sultan Ibrahim of Johore. All races meet on the football field and the well-to-do at golf, tennis and cricket. Two Malays were once playing the grave-diggers in *Hamlet*. Said the first grave-digger: "I'm giving up this job. Ever since Dr. —— has been stationed here, there is no one to bury." Roars of Malay applause greeted this compliment to a popular British footballer. For the liking between Europeans and Malays and between Europeans and Straits-born Chinese is spontaneous and sincere. And hitherto toleration and good-fellowship have marked the intercourse of all the peoples of Malaya, mainly because they had the traditional manners of ancient civilizations—and were too prosperous for jealousies.

CHAPTER III

THE HINDU MILLENNIUM

GEOGRAPHY laid the Malay world open to the influence of the Far East, but down the ages that influence has been confined to commerce and certain skills that commerce brought. It was from Indo-China that the art of casting in bronze and of weaving cotton was carried down through Malaya, and the bronze-workers, who left their drums on the Tembeling and at Klang, bequeathed a large vocabulary to Malaya's aborigines. But the language and habits of China proper were too different to influence the Malays, though (p. 18) envoys from Langkasuka began to visit China as early as the sixth century A.D. For foreigners the Chinese language and calligraphy are difficult and the Chinese have displayed no missionary leanings that might have disposed them to study the language of peoples they despised as barbarian. Chinese monks studied Sanskrit, but that was a sacred language. Modern Chinese, though nearly as clannish as their forefathers, study English, but English is the Open Sesame to material success. It was not China but India that so influenced the spiritual as well as the material life of the Malays that till the nineteenth century they owed nearly everything to her: alphabets, religion, a political system, law, astrology, medicine, literature, sculpture in stone, gold and silver work and the weaving of silk.

The Indians, who built the oldest temples and chiselled Buddhist inscriptions in Sanskrit as early as the fourth century A.D. in Kedah, must have been preceded by traders, who sailed to and fro long before Brahmans and monks and literate adventurers brought the Hindu religion and Buddhism and Sivaite ideas of royalty, and carved Sanskrit inscriptions to which India itself had not long been accustomed. Immigration in larger numbers and permanent settlement began in the first centuries of the Christian era, with commerce as the driving force.

"The contact established between the Mediterranean world and the East after Alexander's campaign, the foundation in India of the empire of Asoka and the later empire of Kanishka, the birth in the West of the Seleucid empire and of the Roman empire gave commerce in luxury commodities a scope deplored by the Latin moralists of the first century. Gold, spices, sandalwood, eaglewood, camphor and benzoin were reckoned among the products of lands and islands beyond the Ganges."

So Professor Coedès in his book *Histoire Ancienne des États Hindouisés d'Extrême-Orient*. And he notes how place-names like Suvarna-bhumi ("Land of Gold") and Suvarna-dvipa ("Islands of Gold") for south-east Asia and the Malay archipelago suggest the probability that above all it was the *auri sacra fames*—"the metal that God chose", as Tomé Pires calls it—which attracted Indians, particularly because migrations in central Asia just before the time of Christ cut the route used by caravans to bring them Siberian gold. Two other accidents stimulated India's overseas commerce: firstly, Buddhism, with its abolition of caste barriers and of the prejudice against crossing the sea and being polluted by barbarian contacts, and secondly the increased size of Indian ships and Chinese junks, built on Persian models, together with the discovery of the Arabs' secret knowledge of the monsoon winds that took those Muslim traders not only to India but, as early as the fourth century, to China.

Yet in spite of having ships that could carry 600 passengers or more, Indians did not reach Malay shores in numbers sufficient to introduce Prakrit, the colloquial form of Sanskrit, or to affect the physical appearance of the local people as Muslim Tamils in the nineteenth century affected the Malays of Penang. Chinese voyagers described the inhabitants of the new settlements not as Indians but as hinduized natives of the Malay world, an account corroborated by the fact that in modern Bali only seven per cent of its Hindu population claim to belong to an Aryan caste. Even so, it took only a Brahminical rite to admit Indonesian chiefs to the second or warrior caste of the Aryan Hindu. To that caste the new kings belonged whether Indians or half-bloods or Indonesian converts tutored by Brahman chaplains in the ritual necessary to turn patriarchal chiefs into incarnations of Hindu gods. As most of the colonists came from the south of India, not all of those Brahmans can have been any more Aryan than the Dravidian Brahmans of the Deccan. But they fixed firmly in the Malay mind a respect for their caste that even now survives unguessed. The Muslim sultans of the Malay peninsula no longer, like the kings of Siam and Cambodia, maintain Brahmans to guard their regalia and conduct court ritual. But in Perak no one outside the royal house may handle the regalia except a hereditary court functionary, the Sri Nara-diraja, whose family may not eat beef and boasts descent from the vomit of Siva's bull, Nandi. At a Perak enthronement it is still this Sri Nara-diraja who proclaims the royal title, and as a Brahman whispers into the ear of his pupil the name of the god who is to be the child's special protector through life, so this representative of past Brahmans whispers to the new ruler the Hindu name of the founder of his dynasty. At the enthronement of a Yang di-pertuan of Negri Sembilan the name of the chosen ruler is proclaimed by a court herald in Brahmanical attitude; that is, by a herald standing on one leg with the sole of the right foot resting on his left knee, his right hand shading his eyes and the tip of the fingers of his left hand pressed against his left cheek.

For the Malay enthronement ceremony, though covered today with a decent Muslim veneer, still retains all the elements of the Hindu ritual. The first rite was lustration. The second was anointing at each quarter of the compass. But wherever Buddhism substituted water for oil, in Burma, Siam and Malaya, there the two rites have been merged. And while in Siam the king turns to every quarter of the globe to be anointed, in Negri Sembilan this has lapsed into a fourfold anointing without change of position. After these rites pious Muslims chant prayers as once Brahmans chanted stanzas of benediction. Next, as so often in Brahman ceremony, there is circumambulation, the ruler being taken in procession round the royal demesne. After that he exhibits himself to his people, wearing in Perak the ornaments of a Hindu god. In the headdress of a Perak ruler is thrust a mediaeval seal, whose handle

THE HINDU MILLENNIUM 27

is made of "thunder" wood; it is called the "lightning" seal, and has taken the place of a symbol of the thunderbolt which Indra always holds as a threat to the wicked. On the Sultan's shoulder is a sword, which in spite of its shape bears the name of the heavy sacrificial dagger "from the heaven-born Ganges", that, inlaid with the figures of Siva and Mahadevi, was used by a famous fourteenth-century ruler of Minangkabau as member of a demon Bhairava sect professing a Tantric doctrine that connected the worship of Siva with the religion of Buddha. While a Perak ruler sits thus enthroned, the Sri Nara-diraja reads an address in corrupt Sanskrit, lauding his Raja's victory over evil, his luck, his justice and his power of healing. Similar addresses are common in India and one is used in Siam. In Negri Sembilan a translation of this formula is read, not by a Muslim dignitary but by one of the court functionaries who must represent the Brahmans of old: it invokes five angels of the sky in place of the Hindu guardians of its five regions who were invoked in Vedic times. A Malay ruler has to sit immobile as possible on his throne, rigidity being evidence in Hindu ritual of incipient godhead.

It was as an incarnation of Siva that Aditiavarman, ruler of Minangkabau in Sumatra, is depicted on his sacrificial dagger, and the founder of Majapahit, last Hindu empire of Java, is sculptured as Vishnu. But it was generally of Indra, controller of weather and lord of Mount Meru the Hindu Olympus, that the rulers of Malay agricultural communities became the receptacle. In Hindu times the capital of Pahang was called Indrapura, city of Indra, and behind the palace at Sri Menanti (in Negri Sembilan) a hill is dedicated to Sri Indra. The rulers of Malacca, Perak and Negri Sembilan claimed descent from the emperors of Sri Vijaya, who at Palembang had a Mount Meru, famous in Malay folklore. The kings of Sumatra, Java, Cambodia, Burma and Siam all had at their capitals a Meru, namely a hill or shrine or temple or palace tower that symbolized the Hindu Olympus. And this symbol was probably identical with the earth-mound that in the time of Confucius stood on the confines of a Chinese town to represent the whole district. The idea of this mound in turn may well have come from Babylon or the Middle East, and have given the Sumatran the idea of a pyramid grave, and the Javanese the idea of a pyramid temple like the Chandi Sukuh, erected when nationalism had revived and triumphed over Indian influence.

The court was the centre of Brahman influence among communities almost entirely Malay. But even the humblest villager could not remain unaffected by an influence that lasted a thousand years. Everywhere, for example, twelve purificatory rites that cleanse a Brahman of original sin have left their mark on the marriage and birth ceremonies of the Malay, on the introduction of an infant to mother earth and father water, on the ceremonies at the beginning and end of his religious studies. Still in remote places the village medicine-man, Muslim though he is, calls upon Siva to restrain malicious spirits from plaguing the sick, from molesting those who would plant rice or build a new house or have killed a deer. But next to the rite of enthronement, the most elaborate Hindu rite is the sacrifice preluding the performance of the Ramayana on the screen of the shadow-play, when, wearing a yellow scarf, the master of the show claims to be an incarnation of Vishnu and makes offerings to Siva the Supreme Teacher and King of Actors and to all the demigods of the Ramayana and Mahabharata.

It is in Kelantan that this rite and plays out of the Ramayana are common, and it is not surprising that the remoteness of this state from foreign influences has favoured the survival of Hindu practices inherited from the oldest centres of Hinduism in the peninsula.

For the first state in Malaya of Indian type was Langkasuka, which, sited in the region of Patani, was for two centuries eclipsed by Fou-nan until India brought it independence and China trade. A Chinese account written in the sixth century says it was then more than 400 years old and had brick walls. Both sexes wore their hair long and wore sleeveless coats made of a cotton (*kipei*) material (*kan-man*), while king and nobles wore pink shawls over their shoulders, gold belts and gold earrings. The women had fine scarves adorned with gems. The king went abroad on an elephant, seated under a white howdah and escorted by drums and banners and fierce-looking soldiers. That there was early Buddhist influence in the north of Malaya is proved by the discovery in Kedah and Province Wellesley of

THE HINDU MILLENNIUM 29

Hinayana and Mahayana inscriptions in Sanskrit that date from the fourth century A.D., and by the discovery at Pengkalan and Tanjong Rambutan in Perak's tin district, Kinta, of two Hinayana (two-armed) Buddhist bronzes of Gupta style that may be assigned to the fifth century. (Alas! the upper portion of the Pengkalan Buddha was lost during the Japanese occupation.) Buddhists evidently were pioneers in colonizing Malaya. But an ornament with Vishnu on a Garuda and a cornelian ring inscribed Vishnu-varmmasya in characters antedating the sixth century have been found at a neolithic shore site at Kuala Selinsing in Perak, and before the end of the fifth century the Sailarajas, or Kings of the Mountain, who ruled Fou-nan, the empire that stretched from Annam to Malaya, had adopted the worship of Siva, who was supposed to descend on the holy mountain from which the dynasty and empire took their names. This was the beginning of the period when Pallavas from the Coromandel coast built little Sivaite temples along the River Bujang (? + ga) in Kedah. Then in the seventh century, after 500 years of domination, Fou-nan fell, leaving it to a Mahayana Buddhist empire, Sri Vijaya, to take swift advantage of the growing commerce from India and Arabia. A Sanskrit inscription setting forth doctrines of Mahayana Buddhism in Pallavan script said to be of the sixth century has been unearthed on the same River Bujang (? + ga) in Kedah. An inscription of A.D. 684 (in the same script but the Malay language) has come down to us from Sri Vijaya's Palembang territory and contains the first dated reference to the existence of this Mahayana Buddhism, or syncretism of Buddhism and Hinduism. According to the monk I-cing, Melayu (later called Jambi) became part of this, the earliest Sumatran Sri Vijaya, between 689 and 692, and so, too, probably Singapore.

The expansion of Sri Vijaya came not with its early unknown dynasty but through the marriage of one of its princesses into a family of Sailendras or Kings of the Mountain who, coming apparently from Fou-nan in the eighth century, ruled central Java, where they built Borobudur and other famous monuments. Before a reaction towards Saivism drove them from Java they had already a footing in Malaya, where in 775 a Sailendra Maharaja left an inscription in Ligor.

And now they created an empire called by the Arabs Zabag or Javaka that embraced not only Kedah and the north of Malaya but the Sumatran colonies of the earlier Sri Vijaya. Apparently the Chinese talk sometimes of Palembang, sometimes of the whole empire, as Sri Vijaya. The roving Malay seamen that were now the subjects of the Sailendras were not of the type to build religious monuments to astound posterity, but their far-flung empire, the Chi-li-fo-che and San-fo-ts'i of the Chinese, greatly impressed Arab voyagers from Oman, who left Abbaside coins dated A.D. 848 at yet another site on the Bujang (? + ga). Arabs tell how the empire of the Maharaja controlled the Sunda Straits from Palembang and the Malacca Straits from Acheh and Kedah. And a copperplate from India records how in 1006 Rajendrachola I of Tanjore granted a charter for a village to support a shrine started at Negapatam by a king of Sri Vijaya and finished by his son Mara-vijayottungavarman—"ray-garlanded sun in the lotus groves of the wise, king of Sri Vijaya and Kedah".

An empire thus strategically placed to control the commerce between India and the Far East was doomed to excite jealous rivalry. In 992 it was attacked by Java and apparently retaliated in 1006. Then in 1025, after a preliminary raid eight years earlier, Rajendrachola I overwhelmed Sri Vijaya and its subject territories, including Melayu (or Jambi) and Lamuri (or Acheh) in Sumatra, along with Kedah and Langkasuka and other places in Malaya. But though the Maharajas had for a time to "worship their conquerors' ankletted feet", Malayan countries were too far beyond "the sounding seas" for the Cholas to hold, and the Arabs again extolled the greatness of an empire that still, in the twelfth century, included Palembang, Acheh, Ligor, Langkasuka, Pahang and Trengganu among its dependencies. But already at the end of the previous century Melayu (or Jambi) appears as a separate kingdom. And soon Java began to encroach on Sumatra and the Thai on the north of the Malay peninsula, and Buddhist power was threatened by Muslim missionaries. By 1281 Jambi was sending to China merchant envoys with the Muslim names Sulaiman and Shamsu'd-din, and in 1292 Marco Polo describes Langkasuka as of no account and talks of eight separate kingdoms in

THE HINDU MILLENNIUM

Sumatra, one of them, Perlak, being Muslim. But the final blow to Jambi, inheritor of the empire of Sri Vijaya, came from Java. As early as 1275 Java claimed Pahang as one of her dependencies, and then at some time between 1338 and 1365 her last Hindu empire Majapahit conquered Sumatra and the Malay peninsula, leaving to this day Javanese words in the Kedah and Kelantan dialects, a Javanese type of creese in Patani and the Majapahit shadow-play in Kelantan. Java dealt the death-blow to the old empire of the Maharajas, and Islam deprived Siva and Buddha of their spiritual ascendancy in the Malay world. One most evil legacy from Sri Vijaya was left to the new age. Rich from international commerce, she had attracted merchants, scholars and adventurers to her ports, but as early as the twelfth century it was said of Palembang: "if a merchant ship passes by without entering, her boats go forth to make a combined attack and all are ready to die (in battle). That is the reason why the country is a great shipping centre." The decline of Palembang into a den of Chinese pirates was a local disaster, but the pattern of sea-power supported by piracy and monopoly that Sri Vijaya bequeathed to Malacca, Portugal and Holland was a cause of war and misery for many lands and countless people.

CHAPTER IV

MALACCA'S CENTURY OF MALAY RULE

BY 1365 Majapahit claimed as a dependency Tumasik, "the Sea Town", or, to use its more famous Indian name, Singapore, "city of the Singhs or lions"; but in a few years that mediaeval haunt of pirates, along with the Malay peninsula, fell under the domination of Siam. It was the murder of Siam's governor of Singapore that drove its Malay king, the Palembang consort of a Majapahit princess, to flee upcountry, where about 1403 he founded Malacca. The legend goes that the site was shown to him by Malay sea-gipsies whose ancestors had served his own as fishermen and pirates in Palembang waters, but it looks as if the Parameswara, or Prince Consort, as the founder of Malacca termed himself in deference to his high-born wife, deliberately chose Malacca as being far enough south not to be overwhelmed by Siam and yet so situated that the port might hope to attract from India, from the east, and from the archipelago the trade that had formerly been enjoyed by Kedah when a part of Sri Vijaya. Kedah, Tomé Pires records in 1512, claimed Malacca, Perak, Manjong, Selangor and Bernam, all of them prized for their tin. Yet Kedah was not only subject to Siam, but apparently part of the little Muslim port-kingdom of Pasai (in modern Acheh), whose missionaries carried Islam inland as far as Trengganu, to judge from a stone there, inscribed in 1326 or 1386 with the first known specimen of Malayo-Arabic script. There is a Megat Kedah mentioned in the chronicles of Pasai, and there is a Pasai grave-stone of 1380 which has been deciphered to refer to a princess of a family that ruled Pasai and Kedah. And the fact that Pasai had a footing in northern Malaya may have influenced Malacca's first ruler to marry a Pasai princess. Whether or not the Pasai house had by intermarriage the blood of the Sailendras who ruled Palembang and Kedah and Acheh is unknown. As early as 1406, according to the Chinese, the Parameswara of Malacca had already claimed the throne of Palembang, and folk-lore has always associated the origin of the Malacca dynasty with Palembang. The second ruler of Malacca assumed the Sailendras' ancient title of Maharaja, and it is to this ruler that the constitution of Malacca is ascribed. That constitution, so far from being based on any Muslim pattern, embodies the ancient Hindu conception of a kingdom as an image of the heavenly world of stars and gods, a conception current in Fou-nan (p. 29) and borrowed probably from Fou-nan by Sri Vijaya. In the ninth century Java was divided into 28 provinces corresponding in number to the houses of the moon, with four chief ministers corresponding to the four cardinal points, and a king, all together making up the number of the 33 gods on Mount Meru, the Hindu Olympus over which Indra presided. Pegu, in the fourteenth century, had 32 governors and a king. Malacca, even as a Muslim Sultanate, had, in addition to the ruler, four great, eight lesser, 16 small and 32 inferior chiefs. From Malacca, Perak and some other modern states have inherited the same constitution.

Sri Vijaya was now to be revenged on the two powers that destroyed its empire. For Malacca proceeded to stem Siamese influence in Malaya and to weaken Java's last Hindu empire Majapahit, both materially by incursions into her trade and politically by encouraging Muslim missionaries to proselytize in Javanese ports.

"Dead we lie wrapped by earth; alive we are wrapped by custom." So runs a Malay saying, and the policy of every Malay state was based on tradition and precedent. As early as the sixth century A.D. Langkasuka, forerunner of Sri Vijaya and later a part of its peninsular empire, had four times sent embassies to China within a hundred years. So now, from Parameswara, founder of Malacca, down to her last Sultan, Mahmud Shah, all the rulers of the new port kingdom sent envoys with tribute to China's new Ming emperors, every one of these Malay potentates seeking recognition of his accession and some of them occasionally asking for protection against Siam.

In 1411 the famous Admiral Cheng Ho, or Ong Sam Po, whom the Malacca Chinese today worship as a minor deity, called at Malacca with a fleet of great junks and took the Parameswara, his consort and followers, 450 people in all, to China, where the Malay prince was entertained by the Emperor in person and given magnificent presents, so mindful must China have been of past trade with the Malay peninsula. The visits of Malacca's rulers to China promoted trade, and the size of China's touring fleets gave Malacca a sense of security.

But closer than Malacca's ties with China were those with India. When its first ruler married in old age the Pasai princess he became a convert to Islam, newly imported from India, and assumed the title of Iskandar Shah, a name illustrious from Islamic legends of Alexander (al-Iskandar) the Great. On his death, as we have seen, there was a reversion to Sri Vijaya's old Hindu title of Maharaja. Then soon after 1445 there was a *coup d'état* at Malacca by Muslim Tamil merchants, who killed an infant ruler of Malay blood royal and elevated to the throne his younger brother by a Tamil mother. This usurper, Muzaffar Shah, was the first ruler to assume the title of Sultan, borne then, Pires says, only by the kings of Pasai and of Bengal. His elevation to the throne gave Tamils a footing in the government of the kingdom which their half-caste descendants lost only on the arrival of d'Albuquerque. There is no doubt that this promoted trade with India, though the Tamil element led to corruption and intrigue.

Malacca, however, emulated not only the commerce but the imperialism of Sri Vijaya and Majapahit. The reigns of Muzaffar and his son Mansur saw the conquest of the whole peninsula south of Kedah and Patani, and across the straits the subjugation of Rokan, Kampar, Indragiri and Siak on the opposite coast of Sumatra. Mahmud, Malacca's last Sultan, conquered Kedah and Patani too, and he ceased to send tribute to Siam and elephants to Java, acknowledging only the suzerainty of China.

Sometimes a conquered ruler fell in battle or was carried a captive to Malacca and his throne given to a Malacca prince. Sometimes he was converted to Islam by the offer of a Malacca princess. As in trade and imperialism, so in diplomacy and administration Malacca followed traditional lines. Her founder had been a Palembang raja married to a princess of Majapahit, which had subjected his country. And just as Siam, for example, had exacted an annual tribute of gold from Malacca, and as Majapahit expected elephants and China pearls and tin, so Malacca required tribute from all her dependencies in return for which they got the protection of her fleets and fighting men. Over the smaller tributaries that had no king, places like Sungai Ujong, Klang, Selangor, Bernam, Bruas and Perak, were set governors with civil and criminal jurisdiction. These governors were given the Sanskrit style of Mandalikas, as Sri Vijaya must have termed them, seeing that a fourteenth-century Trengganu inscription speaks of a Mandalika still in office up the remote Trengganu River. Not till Malacca fell and her governors were supplanted, or as in Negri Sembilan arrogated to themselves independence, did the title of Mandalika die out, surviving only in a few places like Jelebu and Sungai Ujong.

The king of Pahang paid Malacca annual tribute of $5\frac{1}{3}$ lb. of gold, Indragiri and Kampar $1\frac{1}{3}$ lb. each. Other dependencies in Malaya paid tribute in tin. Sumatran states, Rokan, Rupat, Siak and Tungkal paid no tribute but had to supply fighting men at their own cost in time of war. The Celates, or sea-gipsies, of Bintan were required to serve as rowers for certain months of the year.

More important than tribute were the imports that came to Malacca from the countries she subjected, imports that attracted wholesale merchants from Gujerat and Coromandel and Java and China to open warehouses in the port, and brought with the south-west monsoon trading ships from India and with the north-east junks from China. Duarte Barbosa, like all his countrymen, grows almost lyrical over the commerce at Malacca. He tells how there came to the mediaeval port very fine four-masted junks with cargoes of sugar, great store of fine raw silk, porcelain, damasks, brocades and satins, musk and rhubarb, silver and pearls, gilded coffers, fans and other baubles. In exchange for those cargoes the Chinese took away pepper, incense, saffron, coral shaped and unshaped, vermilion, quicksilver, opium and drugs. Four-masted ships with rattan cables and shrouds also came from Java, ships like no

European type, built of very thick timber, so that when the hulls were no longer seaworthy, new planking could be fitted to the old. The Javanese brought for sale finely wrought daggers and spears, gold and the foodstuffs of which, throughout her history, Malacca has always stood in need. In return they carried home cloths from Pulicat and Cambay, opium, rosewater, vermilion, vegetable dyes, silk, saltpetre, iron and drugs. From Malacca ships sailed to the Moluccas for cloves, to Timor for sandalwood, to Bandan for nutmegs and mace. All over the archipelago Malacca distributed Indian cloths, Chinese porcelain, iron knives and drugs. From Sumatra came gold and camphor. Gold, indeed, was so abundant, says Tomé Pires, that the leading merchants kept their accounts in bars of gold, and the richest merchant could discharge three or four ships and reload them from his own stock.

Although they are dated 200 years later, the oldest Malay port regulations extant, coming from Kedah, show that the Malays administered their international ports on lines practised in India from the time of Chandra Gupta to the time of the Great Moguls. They had rules fixing port fees and the duty payable on exports like tin and elephants and on imports like cloth and slaves. They prescribed standard weights and measures, and laid down rules for ships' manifests and the collection by the port officers of money due to trading captains. Tomé Pires records that at Malacca there were four port officers, or Shahbandars, of different nationalities: one for the Gujeratis, the most important of all; one for the Klings, Bengalis, Peguans and Pasai; one for vessels from the Malay archipelago, and one for vessels from China and Indo-China. They presented ships' captains to the Prime Minister, allotted them warehouses, gave them lodgings if they had documents and ordered elephants for them. All shipping from the west, Arabia, India, Ceylon and Pegu, paid fixed dues with presents to the Sultan, the Bendahara, the Temenggong and the Shahbandar for the nation in question. No shipping from the east or the Malay archipelago paid dues; it only gave presents. The value of all cargoes was determined by the Shahbandars, who were "sympathetic to the merchants and of the same nations as the merchants". Or the dues payable on a large cargo might be assessed by a board of ten merchants in the presence of the Temenggong. "The law and the taxes in Malacca were well-known." And though there was some corruption, Malay administration must have been competent and just to foreigners to have attracted so much commerce to the port.

What a change from Parameswara's little village of primitive Malay fishermen, who lived partly at sea and partly ashore among gardens newly planted with bananas, jack-fruit, sugar-cane and vegetables! In less than a century Malacca had grown into a crowded port and the capital of an emperor, whose court was thronged with Indian bravoes, bibulous mahouts with Hindu titles, Tamil merchants anxious to buy their way to royal favour, missionaries of Islam eager to preach the most recent of India's faiths. Decadent that court was now under a weak, clever, half-caste libertine, who would go humbly and on foot to his Arab teacher to seek in mysticism a peace that did not belong to his temporal world, that world where fear made him order the murder of his uncle and of his eldest son, and where he could not save his panders from vengeance or his country from the infidel invader. Yet for a while Mahmud saw Malacca at the height of its achievement and prosperity. According to Duarte Barbosa the Portuguese found it "the richest sea-port with the greatest number of wholesale merchants and abundance of shipping that can be met in the whole world". Neither d'Albuquerque nor Barbosa could ever have realized that already before their time Malacca under its Malay Sultans had played its most important *rôle* in the history of the Far East, and that *rôle* not as a great commercial port but as the place from which Muslim missionaries were to spread over the Malay archipelago and change the lives and ideals of millions of Asiatics for centuries after the commerce of Malacca had become quite insignificant.

For the conversion of Indians to Islam brought to the people of Malacca new intellectual interests on the top of old. The children in its mediaeval streets still knew by heart the Hindu epic of the Ramayana, which Islam failed to banish from the shadow-play that was the cinema of those days. But the educated about the court read or listened to the recital of Muslim historical romances like the tales of Amir Hamzah and

Muhammad Hanafiah, and above all to the story of Alexander the Great, claimed as a hero of the Kuran. The valley of ants, the giraffe-riders, the cave-dwellers with one foot and one eye; the place where angels told their beads above the sun and the noise of that luminary made Alexander faint; the great flies that stoned his troops and were driven away only when one of their number was caught, saddled and mounted by a puppet rider; the angels, who pierced with lances the devils that dwelt in Coptic idols; the bird-worshipping Circassians in tiger-skin tunics; the nude gymnosophists who marvelled that a mortal should bother to subdue a world; Gog and Magog; the diamond mines of Ophir and the copper walls of Jabalqa; the riding on mares into the land of darkness and the visit to the spring of life—these legends of Alexander were more effective propaganda for Islam among an impressionable people, as yet mostly ignorant of the new alphabet, than lessons in difficult Arabic grammar.

Yet, again, the Malay stuck by tradition, turning naturally to the study of Islamic mysticism from the esoteric magical knowledge of the Hindu. So keen was interest in theological speculation that Sultan Mansur Shah sent the Pasai court a present of yellow and purple brocade, a red lory and a brown cockatoo, with a letter offering 9 lb. of gold-dust and two slave-girls to any theologian who could say if those in heaven and those in hell remain in their respective places for ever. Pasai's leading theologian told his Sultan in durbar that they did, but one of his students went to him afterwards and suggested that Malacca would not have propounded a question that was no conundrum at all. He added that his teacher could easily explain that the esoteric answer was not to be blurted out to all and sundry, and he suggested what that esoteric answer was. It must have been the answer given in *The Perfect Man*, a work by al-Jili, a Baghdad mystic who died in 1417, leaving a body of doctrine that spread to the Malays. al-Jili said that the power of endurance in the damned, being a divine gift, extinguished the fire of hell or else their torment changed to pleasure. Islamic romance, Islamic mysticism and Islamic law, all coming from India and tinged with Indian ideas, were first studied in Malacca before being carried to the Moluccas, southern Sumatra, Java, Celebes and Borneo. There is ample evidence that the Malays of Malacca in its brief heyday were neither without the education of the period nor without intellectual interests. Its court was the scene of great literary activity stimulated by many contacts with Java, India and Arabia.

World factors, besides its geographical position, had led to Malacca's success. When it was founded, Sri Vijaya was in eclipse and Majapahit on the way to decay. Malacca enjoyed the fruits of China's maritime trade after the Ming defeat of the Mongols in 1370, and the acceptance of Islam admitted the port to a field of commerce that stretched from Arabia to India.

CHAPTER V

A FAMOSA

PORTUGAL'S expansion overseas began as a riposte to the Moorish invasion of Iberia. Her armadas were built not to challenge the trade or the galleys of Genoa and Venice but as a sailing fleet to challenge the Atlantic. Year by year they ventured farther down the coast of Africa. In 1488 Bartolomeu Dias doubled the Cape. In 1498 Vasco da Gama landed at Calicut, pioneer of the route to India. By the capture of Goa on 25 November, 1510, Affonso d'Albuquerque secured a base from which Portuguese carracks could sail farther east to dispute with paynim kings the produce of the Spice Islands and the trade with the Great Khan.

With that objective the first European ships to reach Malayan waters sailed into the Malacca roads on 1 August, 1509. Their admiral, Diogo Lopez de Sequeira, asked permission to land one of his officers with presents and a letter from King Manuel. The crowd on the beach, never having seen Europeans, took the bearded envoys to be white Bengalis. One of them, a captain, wanting to present the Prime Minister with a gold chain, flung it over his head, a grave insult according to Malay ideas, though the Bendahara passed the incident off, remarking: "Take no notice. These fellows have no manners." Meanwhile, all the Indian merchants urged a Holy War against infidels, of whose interference with Indian trade they had heard alarming reports. A plot was hatched to seize the Portuguese fleet while de Sequeira and his men were being entertained on shore. But a Javanese strumpet revealed the Malay design to her Portuguese lover, and the Malays could only kidnap some 20 Portuguese who were ashore buying cloves. Unable to effect their release, de Sequeira burnt two of his ships for want of crews and sailed away. His errand had served its purpose and provided a *casus belli*.

On 2 May, 1511, d'Albuquerque left Cochin for Malacca with 16 ships (of which one was wrecked on the voyage) and a

force of 800 Portuguese and 300 Malabari fighting men. With
the same fanfare of trumpets and crash of artillery that later
were to affront Canton his beflagged fleet sailed into Malacca
harbour on an evening early in July. There was a pretence of
parley. d'Albuquerque demanded the return of the surviving
Portuguese prisoners. Sultan Mahmud requested him to withdraw his fleet from inshore. d'Albuquerque withdrew his
smaller vessels only, waited six days and then burnt some
houses on the foreshore and all the shipping in the harbour
except Hindu and Chinese junks. At last the Sultan returned
the prisoners, and agreed to pay for all de Sequeira had lost
and to grant a site for a fortress. Communications from the
shore then ceased and the Malays decked their stockades with
flags. The Chinese of the five junks that had been spared said
that beside the Malays Malacca held 20,000 foreign warriors,
20 war-elephants, plenty of artillery, arms and provisions. The
Chinese doubted if it would fall except from starvation.

Neither the size of the port nor the fears of the Chinese
deterred d'Albuquerque. Two hours before dawn, on 25 July,
1511, being St. James's Day, a trumpet sounded on his flag-
ship for the Portuguese captains and men to assemble for confession and absolution before they risked their lives for pride
of arms and greed for trade and, above all, the spreading of
the Catholic faith. The key to their prize was the bridge over the
Malacca River. That bridge gained, the Sultan's stockades and
forces would be divided. Twenty thousand men divided against
1100! But the Portuguese soldiers were disciplined and
fanatical, and their artillery outranged the Malay guns. The
first day of the assault saw a great part of the city burnt and
the mosque and a bridge-head captured, but, his enemy's forma-
tion intact, d'Albuquerque dared not risk a night ashore, and
retreated to his ships with 70 wounded. The *Malay Annals*
relate how, as his enemy retired, the Sultan's son sat on his
elephant indifferent to fire, while an Arab, his religious teacher,
clung to the howdah and begged his young patron to remove
from a bridge that was no place to ponder the unity of God.

The Malays now repaired the stockades on the bridge and
doubled their artillery; they even gave their Javanese mercenaries arrears of pay and three months' pay in advance.

d'Albuquerque, for his part, equipped a tall armoured junk to overtop the bridge he had to take, but the junk at once ran aground and for nine days stuck on a sandbank. Even his grim captains began to be doubtful of success, but before the invincible mind of their Viceroy there was always the vision of Cairo and Mecca deprived of trade and ruined, and of a luxurious Venice that would dine without spices unless she bought from Portugal at Portugal's own price. So on Friday, 8 August, the tall junk was floated and grappled to the bridge. The Portuguese fire overcame the defence. d'Albuquerque landed, and his men being worried by the fire of bombards from the house-tops, he cleared the streets with orders not to spare man, woman or child. The rich port was won. Three thousand pieces of artillery were captured, though the only deaths among the invaders were due to poisoned arrows.

Six bronze lions from some Malay royal grave d'Albuquerque chose for his own tomb. Jewellery and brocaded howdahs and gold-plated palanquins he would have presented to his King Manuel and Queen Maria, along with women embroiderers and many young girls and youths of noble family; but lions and palanquins and embroiderers, all were lost in the wreck of the *Flor de la Mar* off Sumatra.

However, before he embarked on the *Flor de la Mar*, d'Albuquerque took over the Sultan's 1500 slaves and scoured the countryside for fugitive Malays to be put in chain-gangs and set to break up the graves of their bygone kings and, with stone from them and from mosques, to build a great fortress, A Famosa, on the sea-shore. He prepared a commemorative slab with the name of his principal officers, but as they fell out over the order of precedence he turned its graven face inwards over a gateway and on the outer face caused to be carved *Lapidem quem reprobaverunt edificantes*—"The stone which the builders rejected." Having completed A Famosa, issued a new currency in gold, silver and tin, and executed a Javanese headman for seizing the slaves and properties of the Malay chiefs and for trying to corner imported rice, at the end of the year d'Albuquerque left for Goa, lucky to escape with his life from the shipwreck that lost him his lions and palanquins and embroiderers. Communications in those days were so slow that it was 6 June, 1513, before the puissant and invincible King Manuel reported to His Holiness Pope Leo X that Malacca had been captured and was left by d'Albuquerque in charge of 600 of the best soldiers and a well-armed fleet offshore.

Those forces were needed. For here, in hostile seas, the Portuguese stood alone, hated for their cruelty and greed, fighters whose victories never led to friendly alliances, administrators who divided mankind into Catholics, heretics, heathens and Moors, officials deprived of home influences, young, arrogant, dissolute and grasping.

The conquest of Malacca made enemies of the fugitive Sultan Mahmud and his heirs and of their relatives in Perak and Pahang. Frequently, by his fleets or by his influence over Sumatran rulers, Mahmud cut off the food supplies of his former capital. Portuguese ships were captured by Malay warboats, and when some Portuguese landed in Pahang they were given the choice of embracing Islam or being blown from guns. In 1534 Malay warriors killed even a brother of Malacca's Portuguese Captain on the Muar River. In 1586 the Sultan of Johore, one of Mahmud's family, invested Malacca by land and sea, summoning to his aid his house's ancient fiefs, the Minangkabaus of Naning and Rembau, so that the Portuguese Viceroy had to call for loans from Goa Bassein and Chaul in order to equip a force to raise the siege. Punitive expeditions up the Johore River gave only temporary relief. In the end Johore helped the Dutch to capture A Famosa.

Portuguese insistence on monopolies also made her many enemies at Malacca and elsewhere. The first trouble came from the Javanese, who found this new rule irksome after a Malay administration on lines they understood and appreciated for its tact and compromise. When a revolt in the Javanese quarter of the port had been quelled, an attack by 10,000 Javanese from over the sea had to be beaten off. Then came a grave menace from a new power, Acheh. The fall of Malacca and the Portuguese intolerance of all Muslims, as well as their arrogation of monopolies, had attracted to a port that lay outside the range of the Malacca patrol merchants from India, Ceylon and even Turkey, who congregated there in quest of pepper and tin. If

Acheh could oust the European intruder from Malacca, it might hope to step into the place of Sri Vijaya and the Malacca that was.

In 1537, therefore, some 3000 Achinese attempted to surprise A Famosa, only to be driven back from torch-lit ramparts. The worst fright Acheh gave the fort was in 1547, when an Achinese fleet sailed by night into the harbour, caught seven fishermen and, cutting off their noses, ears and feet, sent the Portuguese a challenge written in their blood. "The City was in an Uproar . . . Simao de Mello was as sensible of the King of Acheh's cowardice, as if it had been an outrage; so sacred were the walls of that Fortress, as if to march towards them had been an insolence, to look on them a Crime." But for want of forces Simao de Mello refused the challenge, whereupon St. Francis Xavier, prophesying the timely arrival of two galliots, persuaded some merchants to fit out a fleet. The galliots arrived, and with the improvised fleet set out in search of the Achinese marauders. Meanwhile, the royal cousins of Johore, Perak and Pahang sailed into Muar estuary and stayed three days, to the terror of the Portuguese. But on Sunday morning, while preaching, St. Francis Xavier fell into a trance and saw the little fleet from Malacca drubbing the 20 great vessels of the Achinese away on the Perlis River. In 1551 the mere rumour that a Portuguese fleet had left to harry the harbours of Johore, Perak and Pahang caused the Malays to desert their Javanese allies after they had besieged A Famosa for three months. In 1568 even priests were impressed to help withstand siege by an Achinese armada. As late as 1629 a force from Goa destroyed an Achinese fleet in Malacca River. It seemed there could be no end to the triangular duel between Malacca, Acheh and the Malays, when the exclusion of their ships from Portuguese harbours brought the Dutch to Malayan seas.

For Acheh and Johore caused Malacca such trouble as its Malay Sultans had never seen. Under Malay rule no enemy landed at Malacca, and, their arms always victorious, the Sultans by placating the defeated enlarged their trade abroad and encouraged settlers at home. In return for tribute their fleets protected the countries that acknowledged their sway. Under the Portuguese, Malacca enjoyed few years of peace,

A FAMOSA 45

and its people often had to flee within the walls of the fort for safety. And Portugal gave no return to Asiatics for the taxes wrung from them. Only the Catholic Church cared for the welfare of any Orientals, and then only for the welfare of converts and potential converts. For those converts there was the diversion of watching the pageantry of religious processions as splendid in their way as the pageantry of the former Malay court, with its processions of elephants, bands and umbrellas. In 1551, when good news came from St. Francis Xavier in China, the Captain of the Fort, with men-at-arms, clergy and magistrates, proceeded through decorated streets to Our Lady of the Mount. Four Japanese, brought to see the opulence of nations that worship Christ, were publicly baptized. And the night was devoted to dancing, fireworks and the ringing of bells. In 1567 the whole city turned out to welcome the skull of one of the Eleven Thousand Virgins martyred with St. Ursula. In 1588, when Don Paulo da Lima had destroyed the capital of Johore in revenge for Johore's siege of Malacca, he and his men were greeted on their return by the Bishop and all the clergy, and in the middle of the bridge the victor was crowned with a chaplet of flowers as he knelt in front of a crucifix. Or again, in 1622, when the people were dying of pestilence and famine, there was an efficacious procession of penance to the Church of St. Stephen, where a statue of Nossa Senhora dos Remedios had wept for more than a week.

It was due to Catholic missionaries that in one respect Portugal was in advance of any European rule in Malaya down to the time of Stamford Raffles. It felt and exhibited concern for the spiritual welfare of Asiatics, and in 1548 there was opened a school for the teaching of Portuguese and Latin. Within a few days there were 180 pupils, and the school survived to modern times, to be promoted the College of St. Paul and enter candidates for the Cambridge examinations. Its original pupils must have been only the children of Portuguese, Catholic Eurasians and Catholic converts. But when a Viceroy charged the religious orders with trespassing on the government revenue by continual begging, the clergy could reply that at any rate they did not spend the money on themselves, and that it was official corruption which emptied the public coffers.

Malacca was the scene of St. Francis Xavier's most famous miracles, but when he left it he shook the dust off his feet and ordered the members of the Society of Jesus to abandon a place so wicked.

"When you confess Captain, Factors, or any other officials of the King," wrote St. Francis Xavier, "get complete information of the way they get their living. Ask if they pay taxes, if they make monopolies, if they help themselves with the King's money for their own business and so on. They will answer you that they owe nothing to anybody. . . . Really they are under obligation to restore much to many."

As early as 1514 Tomé Pires wrote that "Malacca should be provided with excellent officials, expert traders, lovers of peace, not arrogant, quick-tempered, undisciplined, dissolute, but sober and elderly, for Malacca has no white-haired official."

The system of government was rapacious and heartless, and it passed on those vices to its officials. Tomé Pires talks of a Malay Bendahara owning 640 lb. of gold, but it is doubtful if any Malay chief made the £20,000 a year taken by the Portuguese Chief Justice from fines and fees, much less the £50,000 and more got by the Captain yearly from perquisites and illegal trade. Spices could be sold only to the Captain's merchants, and a Captain put his merchandise on the King's ships or other vessels without paying freight. Even when customs duties were fixed, the Captains demanded from every ship a huge present, though this was forbidden on pain of excommunication.

But apart from rapacity and corruption, Portugal's empire fell for two cogent reasons. Her population was far too small for empire in any shape. And her hatred of Muslims, which had preserved her in Europe, ruined her trade with Indian and Malay Muslims and added fuel to her perpetual warfare. Acheh, Bantam, Brunai and Patani all wrested from her much of the old Malacca commerce. But nothing can deprive her of the achievement of blazing the way for the coming of the European to Asia, a world event transcending trade figures.

CHAPTER VI

THE DUTCH AT MALACCA

IN the seven years after 1595 no fewer than 65 Dutch ships visited Eastern waters. Then in 1602 the Netherlands, compelling the amalgamation of several smaller companies, gave a monopoly to its famous East India Company, with permission to make settlements and conclude treaties in the name of the government. When a Governor-General was appointed, he lived first in the Moluccas, the spice islands, until in 1619 Jan Pieterszoon Coen, conquering Jakatra in Java, chose Batavia for the Company's capital.

From early days the Dutch company had two objects: to destroy the trade of her competitor, Portugal, on sea, and to capture Malacca, the rival of Batavia for the commerce of the Malay archipelago and the Far East.

As early as 1603 Goa, seat of Portugal's Viceroy, was complaining that the Dutch had seized one of its ships voyaging from San Tomé to Malacca, three or four more ships taking money to Bengal, and off Johore the *Santa Catharina*, richest carrack that had ever left China. The cargo of the *Santa Catharina* was sold at Amsterdam for more than 3,500,000 guilders, and today the Dutch still term the thinnest and finest china "carrack porcelain" after this prize. Early in 1605 another carrack was captured off Patani, the *St. Anthony*, with a cargo of 120 tons of sugar, 268 tons of tin, 223 fardels of Chinese camphor, 90 fardels of agilawood, 18 leaden boxes of musk balls, 11 boxes of vermilion, 22 boxes of Chinese fans, 209 fardels of raw silk and 75 of yellow silk, 6000 pieces of patterned porcelain, 10 casks of porcelain coarse and fine, some gilded couches, benzoin, velvet, woven silk, damask, taffeta and boxes of gold wire. By 1635 the Dutch were intercepting all Portugal's ships, and the trade of Malacca was ruined.

For the capture of Malacca as well as for trade the Dutch, tolerant of Islam and indifferent to all but commerce, tried to keep on good terms with Johore and Acheh. In the very first year of the Company's existence Jacob van Heemskerck was sent to Johore to represent the Dutch as allies against the hated Portuguese. After the capture of the *Santa Catharina*, Johore accepted a Dutch factor and sent two Malay envoys to Holland. In 1606 Admiral Matelief made a treaty promising to help Johore capture Malacca in return for the right of the Dutch to keep the town itself, and to trade with Johore free of duty, and to the exclusion of all other Europeans. The treaty was followed by the first Dutch siege of Malacca, which the threat of a strong Portuguese fleet from Goa caused Matelief to abandon. In revenge, Portugal attacked the capital of Johore. In the next attack on Malacca Johore took no part. The following years saw Johore, Perak, Pahang and Kedah overrun by Acheh, which, carrying on the traditional imperialism of Sri Vijaya, Majapahit and Malacca for the enlargement of her commerce, punished any Malay *rapprochement* with Portugal, the hated rival in trade of all Moors. From 1637 onwards Johore remained the ally of the Dutch, who controlled the Straits of Malacca, and in 1639 their captains were drinking to the man who should be the first Dutch governor of Malacca that year, a toast still premature.

But on 19 May, 1640, at the castle of Batavia, Antonio van Diemen, Governor-General, the Council of India and the Directors of the East India Company announced that from time to time they had considered the capture of Malacca, not only for the expansion of trade but to strengthen influence and prestige over neighbouring princes, and now the moment was opportune as the garrison was weak, the leaders at variance and supplies scarce; also the assistance of Acheh and Johore was expected. As Captain Major to conduct the siege, the Company appointed Adriaen Antonisz, ex-Field-Marshal of their Ceylon campaign. It was recognized that only a strong European army stood any chance of capturing A Famosa, with its walls 32 feet high and 24 feet thick, and its garrison of 260 Portuguese and two or three thousand half-castes and Asiatics. The Dutch blockade of the port started at the beginning of June 1640, but not till 3 August was a landing effected. At first the Captain Major was urged to press the attack vigorously so as to save his

THE DUTCH AT MALACCA 49

troops from the epidemics common during the autumn of fruits and obnoxious smells. But soon it was seen that Malacca was "not a cat to be handled without gloves". The Directors chose a successor to Adriaen Antonisz in case anything should happen to him, reminding him that "all of us are mortal and those nearest the fire get burnt first".

The precaution was not without reason. Both Antonisz and his successor died of sickness. On 5 September the Dutch forces numbered 2283 men on land and sea; by 4 December malaria, plague and dysentery had reduced that total to 1707. Of the 2000 to 2500 Malays of Johore, Naning and Rembau 700 fell sick, but the healthy did much damage to rice-crops, fruits and vegetables, as well as helping in the blockade by sea. So, in addition to sickness, the besieged came to suffer the agony of famine, being driven to eat dogs, cats, rats and the hides of animals. It was estimated that 7000 died. The Dutch sent priests with a white flag to invite surrender. They were driven away from the walls. Letters were then tied to rockets and fired into the city, but to no purpose. At 2 a.m. on 14 January, 1641, a Dutch force of 650 men set out to carry the fort and city by assault. By 10 a.m. that morning A Famosa had fallen. The siege had lasted five months and twelve days and cost the Dutch 1000 men killed in the fighting or carried off by sickness.

The Dutch ascribed the length of the siege to the defection of the Sultan of Acheh owing to a grudge against Johore, to the failure to effect a complete blockade, to epidemics and to the excellent valour of the Portuguese Governor, Manuel da Sousa Coutinho, whom they buried with military pomp two days after the fortress had fallen.

The bastions of A Famosa were given new names: St. Domingo became Victoria, Madre Deos was changed to Emilia, the Eleven Thousand Virgins gave place to Henriette Louise, St. Jago to Wilhelmus, and Courassa, a spacious sea-washed bastion, became Fredrick Hendrick. The bastions no longer bore witness to the glory of God, but to the glory of the sponsors of unmitigated trade, and the walls of A Famosa, ceasing to breathe the enchantment of Rome and the Middle Ages, became a stronghold for ledgers.

As soon as they had captured the port the Dutch considered it their legal right to continue the "tolls, licences and the cruising in the Straits instituted by the Portuguese for the maintenance of the rights of Malacca and now devolved on us by right of conquest".

Import duties were imposed with discrimination of nations and varied from time to time. In some years a higher duty was charged on Portuguese goods than on the cargoes of other nations, but much as Portuguese trade was resented, it was generally esteemed more profitable to let their ships enter Dutch harbours, pay dues and attract customers by their wares, than to drive them to foreign ports. Moors perpetually damaged the Company's trade, so that in 1698 the duty payable by them and other private traders was raised to 20 per cent. In 1699 the import duty on European imports was similarly raised, and later such imports were for a while forbidden. A very important dutiable article was cloth. Rice and other foodstuffs, buffaloes and slaves, if first offered to the Company, were free of duty owing to Malacca's constant need of them.

No ships, unless of a nation specially exempted, could sail in the Straits of Malacca without calling at Malacca and taking out a pass, on penalty of confiscation. At times no passes were granted to Indian ships bound for Acheh and Perak, so that they should have no chance to violate the Dutch monopolies of tin and pepper.

For, another Portuguese right the Netherlands East India Company attempted to exercise was the exclusive purchase at its own price of spices, sandalwood, cloth and tin. But without intermission its tin monopoly was challenged by Achinese, Javanese, Moors and Bengalis, though Dutch cruisers blockaded the coasts of Kedah, Perak and Linggi, and the Susuhunan of Mataram was made to order public floggings for Javanese who tried to run the Perak blockade. Twice the Dutch in a lodge on the Perak River were murdered by Malays who refused to be hectored into selling tin at the Company's low price. Then the decay of Acheh increased the amount of tin sold to the Dutch by Perak, until in 1786 the founding of the free port of Penang killed the Dutch monopoly.

But Kedah, another country that exported tin, was further north and, lying just across the Bay of Bengal, found it easy to

THE DUTCH AT MALACCA 51

evade Dutch restrictions. In 1641 the "modest unpretentious" Sultan promised to refuse Moors entry to his State without passes from Malacca, and to sell half Kedah's output of tin to the Company. Kedah, however, was too close to India and too favoured by the monsoons not to prosecute its trade in tin and elephants with the Muslim and European merchants of India. So the "modest unpretentious" Sultan continued to deal in tin, elephants and calico with ships from Bengal, Coromandel and Java, and to let Moorish cloth be sent overland to Patani, Ligor and Pahang. The Dutch attempt at a blockade was interminable, but the cheapness of the Moorish cloths in Kedah attracted a large Malay and Javanese traffic, and the Dutch consoled themselves by the reflection that if the Moors had not got the trade, it would still have been taken from them by the English, the Portuguese, the French and the Danes.

Like the Portuguese, the Dutch had not yet learnt the need of empire to exclude European rivals from trade and to crush local opposition to monopolies. They wanted no territory other than the port of Malacca, but they had inherited Naning, and its Minangkabau inhabitants had helped them to evict the Portuguese. So at first they demanded nothing from them but a tithe of their rice-crops, which was a foolish and irritating tax in view of Malacca's interminable need of foodstuffs. The Minangkabaus proved so recalcitrant that several Dutch expeditions were sent to exterminate them. But before the Japanese invasion only the Portuguese knew where to fight and where to stop fighting in Malaya. Once 3700 Minangkabaus ravaged Malacca's countryside. At last in place of tithe the Dutch company had to be content with the annual tribute of 400 quart measures of rice, a concession its British successor overlooked to its great cost and shame.

The eternal greed of the Company overreached itself. Holland was drained of men and money, not only by wars in Europe, but by fighting in the East provoked by blockades and piratical methods of enforcing monopolies and diverting trade to her ports. In the middle of the eighteenth century the Company employed, besides 3500 sailors, 18,000 slaves and soldiers, and the army pay-roll amounted to 5,500,000 guilders plus expenditure on forts and factories.

Being more efficient, Dutch exploitation was even more flagitious than the Portuguese. The system was wholly bad, as Raffles recognized so clearly and so indignantly, and it corrupted its agents, whose dishonesty further helped to bankrupt the Company. Officials engaged in private trade, sometimes under fictitious names, and even resigned to sell their experience for high wages under foreign competitors. A young Dutch port-officer at Malacca has described his life there in 1786. "I lead the life of a prince. I live in the finest house in the town and have a nice country-place which I occupy when shipping is slack. I further have a splendid property at Tanjong Kling on which four villages are situated. I cannot tell you the exact number of my slaves but it is over sixty. I have my coach and gig, three sets of horses and two saddle-horses. I have a large office staff. The most arduous part of my task is to receive money and sign my name."

In 1798 the Batavian Republic took over the remaining possessions of a bankrupt Company that with the grossest faults had yet created for Holland a colonial empire and laid the foundations of the Indonesian republic, an achievement that justifies the description "a Dutch period" in the history of South-east Asia.

Malacca, under the Dutch, sank to be the province of a governor, as a capital for the Company's operations had already been opened at Batavia. When it fell into Dutch hands, out of a population of 20,000 only 3000 remained. A quarter of a century later there were 4884 persons living in 137 brick and 583 palm-leaf houses. That total was made up of 145 Dutch burghers, 1469 Portuguese Eurasians and "blacks", 426 Chinese, 547 Moors and Hindus, 588 Malays, 102 Bugis and 1607 slaves.

CHAPTER VII

THE STRAITS SETTLEMENTS

Penang

IN 1592 the first British ship ever to reach the Straits of Malacca anchored off the island of Penang (Betel-Nut Island), where nearly 200 years later the British were to create the first of their Straits Settlements. The ship was the *Edward Bonaventure*, commanded by Edward Lancaster, and she was wrecked and never got home with the pepper, silk, taffetas and Venetian glass that her sick crew pirated from Portuguese vessels bound for Malacca down the halcyon "Ladies' Sea".

A few years later the East India Company had a dozen factories in the Malay archipelago and one at Patani in Siamese Malaya, but unable to withstand competition backed by the Dutch government, or alternatively to share the cost of Dutch forts, troops and fleets, it decided in 1623 to abandon Malayan spices for the calicoes of India. Individual Englishmen, however, continued to drive a large private trade, especially with Kedah, so temptingly close across the Bay of Bengal.

With the great demand for tea (increased by Pitt's reduction of import duty from 100 to 12½% in 1784) there was need not only for a port of call for East Indiamen bound to and from China but for a base with a supply of commodities China would take in exchange, such as tin and pepper, the supply of silver from South America being dependent on political relations with Spain. For these purposes as well as for local trade the advantages of Penang had been urged for years by a young Suffolk trading captain, Francis Light. And in 1785 Light got from the Sultan of Kedah a document leasing the almost uninhabited island to the East India Company with the stipulation that the Company would help him with men, munitions and the loan of money against the attack of any enemy from the interior. The Company guaranteed that the Sultan should suffer no financial loss, and, evidently convinced that money was the real key to possession, appointed Light superintendent of Penang and allowed him to hoist the British flag over it on 17 July, 1786. But in compliance with Pitt's Act of 1784 the Company had to refer to the British Government any agreement that might lead to war, because (after its loss of the American colonies) "schemes of conquest and extensions of dominions" were "measures repugnant to the wish, the honour and policy of the nation". Light had to explain this to the Sultan, but a few months after he had occupied the island he informed Bengal that Kedah feared Siam and that he had told the Sultan the British would assist him! Not till January 1788 did he get the Government's decision vetoing any treaty that might involve military operations against any Eastern prince. Mr. Light "might employ the countenance or influence of the Company for the security of the King of Kedah . . . strictly guarding against any Acts or Declaration that may involve the honour, credit or troops of the Company".

Kedah was to fall a victim to Britain's good intentions. But the Sultan of Kedah did not understand and tried to retake his island by force. Light defeated his quondam friend, and in 1791 a treaty was signed guaranteeing the Sultan $6000 a year for the island, a sum raised to $10,000 a year when, in 1800, Kedah ceded a strip on the opposite mainland (since called Province Wellesley) in order that the British might have complete control of the harbour and a local source of food-supplies.

But Kedah's fear of Siam was not exaggerated. In 1816 she was ordered to conquer Perak for Siam. With commercial impartiality the East India Company sold muskets and gunpowder to Kedah and tried to persuade Perak to send tribute and come to terms with Bangkok. Kedah's conquest of Perak did not placate Siam. In 1821 the state was invaded by the Siamese under the Chau Phya of Ligor, who had recently sent tin to the Governor of Penang and asked for a gun, two or three young "caffre" girls and a pair of handsome spectacles suitable for a man fifty or sixty years old. Malays captured during the invasion were hewn asunder or thrown to crocodiles. Twenty thousand of them fled into Britain's new territory, which the Sultan also reached, scattering rupees from his elephant to delay his pursuers. For the next 20 years His Highness plotted to recover his State with the help of neighbouring Malay rulers and Burma. The Company was not a little anxious about Siam's recognition of its title to Penang, but whenever possible Penang interceded on behalf of the Sultan. Captain Burney, sent as an envoy to Bangkok in 1826, retorted to critics in Penang that no one could negotiate with Siam without means for employing intimidation, that a Siamese viceroy had wanted him hanged for making representations about Kedah beyond his instructions, and that British territory would lose 10,000 Malays if the Sultan were restored. In 1827 the Penang government asked the Recorder if the order of the Governor-General was legal justification for the use of arms to remove to Malacca a Sultan whose plotting had long embarrassed its neutrality. Sir John Claridge, the Recorder, in a minute "altogether unprecedented and unbecoming", gave his opinion that whether warranted or not, such a proceeding would disgrace the British and he would not have his name mixed up with it. Several times the Sultan's adherents attacked the Siamese in Kedah in vain. But the Chau Phya of Ligor died and Siam grew tired of unprofitable guerilla wars. In 1842 Sultan Ahmad Taju'd-din's persistence was rewarded and he was allowed to return to Kedah as its ruler. But the government of Kedah remained mediaeval, until in 1905, Kedah being on the verge of bankruptcy, Siam appointed a British adviser, who induced the Sultan to appoint a State Council. In 1909 Siam transferred its suzerainty over Kedah to Great Britain.

As for Penang, apart from these foreign relations, its early history is the sorry record first of amateurish and then of extravagant administration. It is now a constituent State of the Federation.

Malacca

Meanwhile European politics had given Great Britain a hold over Malacca 30 years before it became British territory. For after the French Revolution an alliance between France and a Batavian Republic made every Dutch fort in the East

Indies a potential base for French warships, so that to safeguard her own possessions and conserve those of her ally, the exiled Stadtholder, Great Britain took over Malacca and later seized Java by force of arms. The Dutch Governor of Malacca entertained the British officers to dinner after their arrival, and when he left, "the council deemed indispensable for legal administration was retained against its will". But expecting to have to hand Malacca back to the Dutch, the East India Company spent two years and thousands of pounds on demolishing that perfect specimen of a mediaeval fort, A Famosa, in case Britain might ever have to attack the settlement! The Directors even talked of removing the 15,000 inhabitants to Penang, so that never again might Malacca be the rival of that northern port. Fortunately, in 1808 Thomas Stamford Raffles, later the founder of Singapore, went on a holiday from Penang to a place in which Malay research had interested him, and he dissuaded the Directors by a report on Malacca's valuable buildings, its cultivated fields and its constant revenue, and by a plea that the people considered British faith pledged for their protection. After the downfall of Napoleon, the Convention of London in order to strengthen Holland in 1814 returned Malacca (and Java) to her, but it was not till 1818 that the Dutch took Malacca back, and then in 1824 the Treaty of London ceded it finally to Great Britain, His Netherlands Majesty engaging never to form any establishment in Malaya.

The history of British Malacca is the history of its administration and of war with Naning (p. 79), the little Minangkabau state on its boundary. Though in 1801 the English had made a treaty (voidable, if the Dutch returned) with Naning as at least a semi-independent tributary State, an industrious Superintendent of Lands, Mr. Lewis, wrongly told Governor Fullerton that Naning was part of Malacca territory and that revenue was being lost by the remission of a tithe of its large rice-crop. Perhaps Dutch merchants in Malacca spread rumours disturbing to Naning, in the hope of reaping the profits of a war. Anyhow, the fears of the Penghulu (or chief) of Naning were aroused, and he ended by claiming absolute independence. So in July 1831 150 sepoys with two six-pounders dragged by bullocks were despatched to Naning, but were bogged and had their retreat stopped by the felling of trees in their rear, until with guns and baggage lost the red-coats had to retire "expeditiously" to Malacca, where "fear whispered that every bush concealed a Malay and converted every stick into a musket barrel". The safe retreat of the sepoys was in fact due to the adroitness of a Malay leader, who having saved his State considered it absurd not to accept $500 to let the enemy get back to Malacca as soon as possible. Jubilant, Penghulu 'Abdu'l-Sayid of Naning now complained that the sepoys had shot a warrior sent to escort the Assistant Resident, and he sacrificed on the warrior's grave six out of seven Malaccan convicts captured during the "war", keeping the seventh to read the Kuran to him. He also wrote to the King of England a letter of protest.

Too late the officials at Malacca discovered that Naning was within its rights in objecting to any tithe, the Dutch having commuted it into nominal tribute since 1765. But now jungle warfare, with its uncertainties, was inevitable. To keep open a way of retreat, a road 600 feet wide was cut at the rate of three or four miles a month over the 22 miles to Naning. Even so, the British Colonel was nervous, complaining of "troops knocked up" and acting on the defensive against enemies who never numbered more than 100 men. The Penghulu of Naning swore to hamstring all the buffaloes of anyone who supplied the British with transport. In the end, a force of friendly Malays from Rembau surprised the Penghulu at his dinner and broke the Naning defence. Promised a pardon, Penghulu 'Abdu'l Sayid was given a pension and a house in Malacca, generosity that impressed the Malays more than the British tactics in an unjust and petty campaign.

Like Penang, Malacca is now a State in the Federation.

Singapore

Thomas Stamford Raffles, the founder of Singapore (formerly the most important of the Straits Settlements), was born at sea off Jamaica on 6 July, 1781, the son of a sea-captain of such narrow means that his mother once complained of the boy's extravagance in burning a candle over his books. At the age of fourteen Raffles entered India House as an extra clerk. Ten years later his talents won him the appointment of Assistant Secretary to the Presidency of Penang at £1500 a year. Unlike most of his colleagues, he took the pains to study Malay, and by temperament he was interested in the abolition of slavery and in Britain's responsibility for the welfare of her Asiatic subjects. In 1808 he urged on the Directors our moral obligations towards the people of Malacca. He added that from their territory Great Britain might render the Rulers of the Malay States "not only subservient but, if necessary, tributary". In 1810 he was posted to Malacca as Agent for the Governor-General to prepare for the British expedition against Java. Until it was returned to Holland in 1814 he was Lieutenant-Governor of that island. After that he went on leave to England, when at a levee the Prince Regent praised Raffles' book on Java for 20 minutes and knighted him. His next office was that of Lieutenant-Governor of Bengkulen, a derelict spot but the one British possession in the Malay archipelago. It was, as he remarked, an Elba on which he was not secure, though he failed to get support for his scheme to extend British territory in Sumatra. In October 1813 he visited Lord Hastings at Calcutta and got permission to look for a spot for a British station at Riau (Rhio) or in Johore. "There is some reason to think," his instructions continued, "that the Dutch will claim authority over the State of Johore by virtue of some old engagements, and though it is possible the pretension might be successfully combated, it will not be consistent with the policy or present views of the Governor-General in Council to raise a question of this sort with the Netherlandish authorities." The Dutch had anticipated Raffles at Riau, and the Carimon (*Kĕrimun*) Islands a marine survey condemned as unsuitable.

So on 28 January, 1819, he landed at Singapore, where the local hereditary chief, the Temenggong (direct ancestor of the present Sultan of Johore), told him that there were no Dutch and that the British could buy land for a factory there or in Johore. But the Temenggong was a subject of his cousin, the Sultan of Riau, Lingga, Johore, Singapore and Pahang. That

Sultan, 'Abdu'r-Rahman, was under Dutch surveillance and would certainly be forbidden to ratify any cession to the British. 'Abdu'r-Rahman, however, was a younger son, enthroned by *Bugis* influence immediately after his father's sudden death in 1812, while Husain, the elder son, protégé of the two greatest *Malay* chiefs, the Temenggong of Johore and the Bendahara of Pahang, was away in the Malay peninsula marrying the Bendahara's daughter. Raffles himself in 1813 had recognized 'Abdu'r-Rahman, but now to secure a good title to Singapore he decided to install Husain as Sultan of Johore. On 30 January, 1819, the Temenggong in his own name and that of Sultan Husain agreed to let the East India Company select land for a factory at Singapore or in Johore in return for an annual grant of $3000. Fetched from Riau, Husain was installed Sultan of Johore at Singapore on 6 February and confirmed the Temenggong's preliminary agreement, the annual grant being raised to $5000 for the Sultan and $3000 for the Temenggong, and "factories" substituted for "factory".

The Malay chiefs had been eager to make money out of an almost uninhabited mangrove swamp and they had probably heard of Raffles' fair dealings with Asiatics, but as the Dutch had returned to power, and as the British had given way before them for two centuries, it was clearly an occasion for diplomacy, especially as rumour said that Batavia was sending troops for Timmerman Thyssen, the Dutch governor of Malacca, to attack the English at Singapore. They wrote to Riau and Malacca that Husain had been forcibly installed. Timmerman Thyssen, though he did not attack, protested to Bannerman, Governor of Penang, that the Temenggong on behalf of Sultan 'Abdu'r-Rahman had signed an agreement with the Dutch on 26 *November*, 1818, by which Riau and Lingga were to be free ports, but all other harbours in the Sultan's kingdom were to be free only to Dutch and local vessels. That treaty in Raffles' eyes was invalid, because when quitting Malacca in 1795 its Governor, Couperus, had declared that Riau, Lingga, Johore and Pahang were not its dependencies, so that no prior right now justified them in spurning the agreement Riau had signed with the British on 19 *August*, 1818, promising not to renew any treaty that might obstruct British trade at any port in those countries. But Bannerman, the Governor of Penang, was too jealous of Raffles and a rival settlement, and too apprehensive of Dutch power not to admit Holland's pretensions. He refused to risk adding "violence to injustice" by sending troops to Singapore and he wrote to Lord Hastings advocating withdrawal. To the Dutch Lord Hastings wrote a diplomatic letter expressing unfeigned regret at the occupation of the port, explaining how too late he had tried to prevent Raffles from forming any British establishment, but concluding that abandonment now would imply "subscribing to rights which you claim and of which we are not satisfied, thereby awkwardly forestalling the judgment which was to have taken place at home".

Bannerman received a stern rebuke. Jealousy of "the new post, should misfortune occur and be traceable to neglect originating in such a feeling, will find no tolerance with this Government, who must be satisfied (which is not now the case) that perseverance in maintaining the post would be an infraction of equity before they can consent to abandon it". So Bannerman had to send 200 troops to Singapore.

On 14 August, 1819, the Company's inner cabinet decided that Raffles had contravened the spirit of his instructions and, should the Dutch expel the British garrison from Singapore, England must either submit or hazard a war that might involve all Europe. But the Directors took no other action and awaited an explanation from Lord Hastings, who, primed by Raffles, became more impressed with the value of the new port and with Holland's "injurious policy" of monopolies than by the validity of her claim to Singapore. Controversy raged until the Anglo-Dutch treaty was signed at London on 17 March, 1824, though long before then the amazing growth of Raffles' political child had convinced India House not only of the commercial value of the island but of a moral obligation to hold it.

By June 1819 the influx of Chinese, Bugis and Malacca Malays had raised the population of Singapore to 5000, and a year later that figure had doubled. The exports and imports by Asiatic crafts alone exceeded $4,000,000 for the first year. But this was only a beginning. The history of Singapore is written mainly in statistics, and to them the student of its development turns for comparative figures of its trade, which are startling:

	Singapore £	Penang £	Malacca £	Total £
1825	2,610,440	1,114,614	318,426	4,043,480
1850	5,637,287	1,644,931	439,175	7,721,393
1864	13,252,175	4,496,205	821,698	18,570,078

Raffles himself saw Singapore only as a mangrove swamp when he first negotiated for a site there, and once more when he stayed there from October 1822 until 6 June, 1823, to draw up plans for its future with "trade open to ships and vessels of every nation free of duty, equally and alike to all". It was after he had left the East for ever that on 2 August, 1824, the whole island was ceded to Great Britain. The lamentable vagueness of the arrangement with Kedah over the leasing of Penang was not forgotten. It was definitely laid down that neither Great Britain nor Johore should be bound to interfere in the internal concerns of the other's government or in any political dissensions or wars within their respective territories or to support each other by force of arms against any third party. Fortunately Holland gave no cause for the British to test the validity of these professions.

Singapore from its foundation down to the time of the Japanese invasion was a scene of peaceful commercial development, disturbed only for a few years by pirates who molested its sea-traffic and by pitched battles among Chinese Secret Societies, which in 1854 resulted in the killing of 4000 Chinese in ten days. This private piracy of the nineteenth century was no more than a relic in the tradition of the national piracies which for centuries had enforced monopolies that deprived the Asiatic of a proper price for his produce. And before judgment is passed on the method of its acquisition, it must be remembered that to Raffles the creation of the free port of Singapore was far more than a bid for the extension of British commerce. In the present century free trade is only an economic doctrine: to Raffles it was a battle-cry for the rights of the Asiatic man.

CHAPTER VIII

BRITAIN AND THE MALAY STATES

DOWN the centuries the Malay States of the peninsula were fated not to coalesce or for long to co-operate. First, Majapahit and Siam broke the power of the Malay Buddhist empire of Sri Vijaya which from Kedah held the northern states together for five centuries. Malacca, succeeding Sri Vijaya, conquered and controlled the peninsula for less than a century. Then the Portuguese conquest cut off the north of Malacca's newly won empire from the south, leaving Kedah, Kelantan and Trengganu to become distant tributaries of Siam, and Perak (a State founded by the eldest son of Malacca's last Sultan) to be conquered by Acheh. Also, though apart from its quarrel with Islam Portugal took no interest in Malayan politics, its conquest of Malacca was to lead to the rise of two races destined to hew two pieces out of the Johore empire that was the relic of Malacca's empire. For, hating Muslims, the Portuguese encouraged the then Hindu Minangkabaus of Sumatra to immigrate into the valleys that the eighteenth century saw turned into an independent Negri Sembilan under a Minangkabau prince. And driving trade away from the Malacca Straits by their patrols, the Dutch rivals of the Portuguese brought wealth and enterprise to the Bugis of Macassar, who at the end of the seventeenth century founded the kingdom of Selangor. Even when they had conquered the Portuguese, the Dutch still had no imperialist leanings, but in the absence of their economic patrols the Bugis from Selangor might have become the suzerains of all the Malay States instead of having to be content with the virtual control of the Johore empire from Riau and with winning high offices in Kedah and Perak by force of arms. In the end the Dutch quashed Bugis ambitions and destroyed the Bugis chance of dominating the Malay States.

Then, in 1824, the Treaty of London allotted to Great

BRITAIN AND THE MALAY STATES 63

Britain the Malay peninsula and to Holland all the islands lying to starboard of East Indiamen voyaging to China, an accident of alien politics that split the remnants of the Johore empire for ever. To the Johore Sultanate was left only the Riau archipelago, while the two greatest Malay chiefs of the broken empire were cut off at Pahang and Johore from their overlord in the Riau area, and soon made themselves independent Sultans. The ties between the Bugis rulers of Selangor and the Bugis Underkings at Riau were also severed. Lack of communications and sequestering forests had always made for separatism with narrow local loyalties, and now that there was no suzerain to arbitrate or command, fratricidal quarrels broke out in Perak, Negri Sembilan and Pahang, and there was anarchy in Selangor. In the '30s of the last century Negri Sembilan saw five claimants to its throne. In 1857 Wan Ahmad, afterwards first Bendahara Sultan of Pahang, started a six years' war against his brother for possession of that country. The general anarchy infected the growing Chinese population. At Lukut Chinese miners rose and murdered the heir to the Selangor throne, thrusting his wife and children back into their burning house. In a struggle between Selangor chiefs a Straits-born Malacca Chinese, Baba Tek Cheng, supplied the sinews of war, requiring only interest on his outlay until victory should put his man in a position to grant limitless concessions of land.

The many quarrels, intricate and petty but disastrous to welfare, have no interest today. But in the midst of the anarchy, the Singapore Chamber of Commerce was informed on 21 August, 1872, that "it is the policy of Her Majesty's Government not to interfere in the affairs of the Malay States unless where it becomes necessary for the suppression of piracy or the punishment of aggression on our people or territories; and that if traders, prompted by the prospect of large gains, choose to run the risk of placing their persons and properties in the jeopardy which they are aware attends them in these countries under present circumstances, it is impossible for Government to be answerable for their protection or that of their property".

Things got worse. In the fighting at Kuala Lumpor between a Raja Mahdi and the Sultan's progressive Kedah son-in-law,

Chinese partisans paid so much a head for the corpses of adherents to the side they did not favour, and an Arab mercenary captured 80 sepoys with two European officers, of whom one was killed in the fighting and the other had his throat cut as Muslims slaughter buffaloes. Pahang joined in the fray.

In the State of Perak, faction fights had started among 40,000 Chinese miners in Larut, whose Malay chief grudged wasting any of his annual revenue of $200,000 on such a novelty as regular police. When he did recruit a small force, it was manhandled by some professional Chinese fighting-men he had hired to deal with the miners. Chinese throats were cut to dye the banners of the victorious side. Hundreds perished in the fighting. In vain the Malay chief, the Mantri, trimmed to be on the side of the faction for the moment victorious. There was piracy along the Perak coast and there were clan-fights in the streets of Penang.

Meanwhile on the Perak River a Sultan's body lay unburied for a month until the chiefs settled the claims of two rival Perak Rajas for the throne by electing a foreign Raja, Isma'il, connected with the ruling house by marriage only.

Once again the leading Chinese merchants of the Colony sent a petition to the Governor contrasting the peacefulness of Johore and the order in the northern States under Siamese suzerainty with the lawlessness and turbulence in the other Malay States. For the British not to intervene in "the half-civilized States of the Malay Peninsula (whose inhabitants are as ignorant as children), is to assume an amount of knowledge of the world and an appreciation of the elements of law and justice, which will not exist among those Governments until your petitioners and their descendants of several generations have passed away". A little arrogant and condescending, but then the Malay of those days thought no more than a tiger thinks of killing a Chinese. To the Chinese the Malay was a barbarian without culture; to the Malay the Chinese was a pagan without rights.

It was the complaints of the Chinese and fear lest some other European power might get a footing in the Malay States that now led the Secretary of State for the Colonies to execute a

BRITAIN AND THE MALAY STATES 65

complete *volte-face*, as Downing Street has so often done in its Malayan policy. A despatch dated 20 September, 1873, informed the Governor of the Straits Settlements that:

"Her Majesty's Government have, it need hardly be said, no desire to interfere in the internal affairs of the Malay States; but, looking to the long and intimate connection between them and the British Government . . . Her Majesty's Government find it incumbent to employ such influence as they possess with the native princes to rescue, if possible, these fertile and productive countries from the ruin which must befall them if the present disorders continue unchecked.

"I have to request that you will carefully ascertain, as far as you are able, the actual condition of affairs in each State and that you will report to me whether there are, in your opinion, any steps which can properly be taken by the Colonial Government to promote the restoration of peace and order and to secure protection to trade and commerce with the native territories. I should wish you, especially, to consider whether it would be advisable to appoint a British officer to reside in any of the States. Such an appointment could, of course, only be made with the full consent of the native Government."

A new governor, Sir Andrew Clarke, arrived in Singapore within three months of this change of policy, and in less than a year he had got Perak, Selangor and Sungai Ujong to accept British advisers.

The instrument employed to needle the way into Perak was the Raja Muda 'Abdullah, the legitimist heir to the throne, whom the chiefs had passed over for the foreigner Isma'il. 'Abdullah was ready to sign any document if he could be made Sultan, and it was easy for him to persuade chiefs favourable to his cause to come to Pangkor and sign too. The treaty, executed on 20 January, 1874, was not by any means the success those concerned liked to think it. The deposed Isma'il, though given a title and a pension of $1000 a month, was not

C

amused. The cession of the Dindings to Great Britain at the instance of one of 'Abdullah's Chinese creditors was suspected to be the prelude to the total annexation of Perak. The Mantri of Larut, who considered that 'Abdullah had some time ago made him an independent ruler with the subsequent approval of the British, was chagrined at becoming his subject and having to foot the Colony's bill for disturbances in Larut which 'Abdullah had fanned. He paid a lawyer $12,000 to place his case before Parliament, but dropped the matter on the order of 'Abdullah, who feared for his new throne.

The sequel to this unpropitious beginning was lamentable; the entry of the British into the Malay States being as ill-starred as the acquisition of the first of the Straits Settlements. James Wheeler Woodford Birch, whose career had been mainly in Ceylon, was ignorant of the Malay saying, "When you enter a byre, low; when you enter a pen, bleat," and he dashed into Perak like a Victorian rationalist schoolmaster, confident that decision and firmness would soon remedy abuses. Chiefs who had depended for their livelihood on the collection of taxes in hereditary areas were termed blackmailers and threatened with legal proceedings instead of being paid or promised compensation for the loss of those rights. Complacently Mr. Birch wrote to the Governor at Singapore, "It concerns us little what were the old customs of the country, nor do I think they are worthy of any consideration." One of those old customs was slavery, but, without awaiting legislation or offering compensation, Mr. Birch, acting from a generous heart rather than a diplomatic head, abetted the escape of fugitives regarded by their owners as legitimate and valuable property.

Before the end of 1874 'Abdullah sent a secret message to the deposed Sultan Isma'il: "If Mr. Birch asks you for the regalia or desires to install me, do not consent. Should you consent to my installation as Sultan, Perak will be given over to the English; for my words have caused me to be much indebted to them. Should I myself ask for the regalia in the presence of Mr. Birch, do not consent to give them up." Mr. Birch explained his programme for future taxation to a gathering of chiefs. In the words of one of the Sultan's retainers, the Malays concluded that "he had nothing to fill his belly and came to Perak to collect the revenue of others". 'Abdullah sent a deputation to the Governor at Singapore. There were grievances over minor matters such as the Resident's arbitrary fixing of a district boundary against the weight of local evidence. But the chiefs decided to confine their complaint to important issues. They wanted Sir Andrew Clarke to forbid Mr. Birch to interfere with religion and custom and to counsel him to consult Sultan and chiefs, and not to deprive them of feudal dues, at present their only source of income, or to assist the escape of slaves, their property by custom 3000 or more years old. Sir Andrew was retiring and handing over to his successor. Nettled by the Sultan's action, he told the deputation never to bring the Governor letters that had not been seen by the Resident, and he wrote to 'Abdullah to obey the Governor, describing himself as one "who lifted you out of your misery and sorrow, giving you position and honour" and Mr. Birch!

There was now a meeting of chiefs who talked of poisoning the Resident but finally accepted an offer of the Maharaja Lela to stab him. The Sultan, however, consulted a lawyer as to legal means for his removal and tried to borrow $5000 from the Lieutenant-Governor of Penang in order to buy a diamond star for the Governor's impending visit. Having failed to get the loan, His Highness approached Mr. Birch, who seized the occasion to arrest one of the Sultan's boatmen for past rowdyism in a native theatre. This affront was the last straw. The Sultan sent for the state wizard to call up the guardian genies of Perak and enquire if they would wreck Mr. Birch's steamer on the river-bar and destroy him. The Sultan was one of the mediums, and stabbing a flour mannikin repeatedly declared the Resident would be dead within a month. Another medium was paid $100 to produce Mr. Birch's spirit of life in the form of a butterfly, which was killed with a knife.

The new Governor seems to have had a better idea than the Resident of how to handle people three centuries behind the times, although unfortunately he was even less inclined to move cautiously than his predecessor. He visited Perak and received the Sultan (complete with Star), surrendering to him two fugitive slaves with a lecture on debt-slavery and a proposal that the Perak chiefs should receive allowances and hand over government to the British. Two rajas, Yusuf and Idris (both destined to be Sultans) accepted this offer. So did 'Abdullah later. Elated by this victory, Mr. Birch drafted a far more stringent agreement than the Governor had proposed, and told the Sultan that if he did not sign it the throne was to be given to Raja Yusuf. 'Abdullah yielded, but Raja Yusuf advised that troops should be summoned before the proclamations as to the new system of taxation were posted. 'Abdullah sent a handsome creese to the Maharaja Lela at his village Pasir Salak, a symbolic acceptance of his offer to stab the Resident. Three days after his assassins had been appointed, Mr. Birch, with a sprained ankle, sat in his house-boat at Pasir Salak and ordered his clerk to post the proclamation abolishing the collection of taxes by any authority but the British. The Malays tore down the notices, stabbed the clerk and speared Mr. Birch through the flimsy palm-leaf walls of a bath-house. The date was 2 November, 1875.

More than a thousand troops were despatched from India to hunt down the murderers and their abettors. Three chiefs were hanged, and 'Abdullah with two others was banished to the Seychelles. When, more than twenty years later, the ex-Sultan had returned and I met him, an elderly dandy in European clothes, he helped out my still halting Malay with excellent English, and pointing to the Sultan's fine palace and motor-cars, ejaculated, "Had I but foreseen!"

The Executive Council of the Straits Settlements was instructed to hold an enquiry into the Perak tragedy. It found that, in spite of admirable qualities, Mr. Birch had sometimes acted injudiciously without respect for Malay customs and in an overbearing manner. Especially it deprecated his interference with feudal taxation before allowances had been fixed to compensate chiefs for their loss.

But it took several years before Perak settled down. The Maharaja Lela did not surrender until July 1876, and was not hanged until 20 January, 1877. As late as June 1876 Mr. Davidson, the local lawyer appointed as the successor of Mr. Birch, had to be informed by the Governor that his proposal to settle in a stockade with 50 or 60 troops would be an undignified confession of failure. Perak was bankrupt and the Malays sullenly hostile. The troops could not stay indefinitely. It was decided to replace them with 800 police, mostly Malays, but no one knew how they were to be paid. Mr. Davidson resigned.

The next Resident, Mr.—afterwards Sir—Hugh Low, had been a botanist, and was now to provide the model for the administration of all the protected Malay States. How much of his policy was original, how much due to the Governor and how much to Downing Street has not yet been explored. It was now recognized that to govern a people by intimidation is an expensive and unsatisfactory course. The cost of a police force was reduced by giving police duties to headmen and abolishing many village police-stations. To compensate them for loss of feudal taxes the chiefs were given administrative posts and a substantial percentage of the government revenue collected in their districts. Land rents took the place of forced labour. A State Council was started on the model of Indian Councils created by an Act of 1861, after the Indian mutiny had taught us the need of bodies competent to interpret the wishes of the people. All revenues were collected, all appointments filled and all land alienated in the name of the Sultan. The Sultan was also President of the Council, on which sat the British Resident, the major Malay chiefs, and Chinese business men. Under the strict Muslim constitution of former days the Chinese had had no rights at all, not even the right to possess land. Now they were not shy to express their views even on the merits of candidates for the throne of Perak. They objected strongly to the appointment of Sultan Yusuf, until Sir Hugh Low declared that it would be embarrassing to tell Queen Victoria her nominee was rejected. "Oh!" said the Chinese. "Why did you not tell us before that Queen Victoria wants him? If Her Majesty recommends him, he must be suitable."

The Malays of those days were not yet qualified for official posts, but their views were consulted and their local knowledge was of inestimable value. In six years the Perak debt of $800,000 was paid off, and in 1883 slavery was abolished. The population roughly estimated in 1879 at 81,084 souls was found by 1891 to be 214,254.

After getting the Perak chiefs to sign the Pangkor treaty,

the Governor at once turned to Selangor, where civil war and piracy had long been rife, though the immediate excuse for his interference was the murder of eight British subjects from Malacca at Kuala Langat by pirates disguised as fishermen. The pirates were the followers of the Sultan's third son. The Sultan, a rather careless philosopher, whose interests were gardening and hoarding tin, readily agreed to the trial of the offenders, explaining that piracy was not his affair but the affair of his boys, and sending a creese for the execution of those found guilty.

A liking for the English as rivals of the Dutch was a Selangor tradition, and now Selangor chiefs, whether out of politeness or conviction or owing to the presence of a British naval squadron, expressed the desire to have a Resident. Sir Andrew Clarke, however, was content to leave a young civilian, Frank Swettenham, to give the Sultan informal advice. The Sultan soon reported to the Governor that the young man knew the customs of the country and was clever at winning hearts with soft words, so that all men rejoiced in him as in the perfume of an opened flower. His Highness wanted to pay Mr. Swettenham's salary and expenses. The Governor now appointed a Resident, Mr. J. G. Davidson, a writer to the signet, who afterwards succeeded Mr. Birch in Perak. Mr. Swettenham, energetic, tactful and of great promise, remained with the Sultan at Langat as Assistant Resident. One item in Selangor's earliest budget was $300,000 owed by the Sultan's son-in-law to a Chinese in Malacca for munitions for the civil war that had rent the country. In extending British protection over Selangor there was no trouble, evidently owing to the tact of a young civilian who was to retire in 1903 as Governor of the Straits Settlements, and to die in London in 1946 at the age of ninety-six, combatting in the very last weeks of his life a Malayan Union which he regarded as a stupid betrayal of the race he had served so well.

To extend protection over Negri Sembilan, the Nine Counties, by one treaty was impossible, as each of the larger claimed to be independent. In April 1874 the most important of the territorial chiefs, the Dato' Klana of Sungai Ujong, along with the Dato' Muda of Linggi, signed a bond in

$50,000 not to infringe the peace with arms given them in order to clear the Linggi River from the evil-disposed persons who built stockades and hindered traffic by unlawful exactions. They also promised not to harbour enemies of the British Government or of its friends. In return "the moral and material guarantee and *protection*" of Great Britain was to be accorded them "to secure the *independence*, peace and prosperity of Sungai Ujong". This cryptic document was followed by the hoisting of the Union Jack at the Klana's house. But an old chief of Sungai Ujong, the Dato' (Shah) Bandar, threatened trouble, ostensibly because the Klana had not consulted him. Next, when the Dato' Bandar had surrendered, the Yamtuan Antah of Sri Menanti and other chiefs attacked the Dato' Klana. A British force of 150 infantry and a detachment of artillery dealt with this disturbance, a British officer, Captain Channer, winning a V.C. for leaping over a stockade into the jaws of the unknown and driving a few Malays away from their cooking-pots.

By January 1876 military forces were withdrawn from everywhere except Sungai Ujong. All the chiefs supporting the Yam-tuan Antah went with him to Government House and promised to refer any disputes for the arbitration of Maharaja (later Sultan) Abubakar of Johore. For the British Government was unwilling to appoint any more Residents after what had happened in Perak until it had "had further experience of those already established". So with the approval of Singapore, the ambitious Maharaja of Johore sent a representative "as a sort of Resident" to Sri Menanti, the seat of Yam-tuan Antah. But Johore failed from its ignorance of the matrilineal organization. Squabbles among chiefs continued in Rembau and Jelebu. But when Jelebu applied for a British Resident to arbitrate, the Governor decided it was inexpedient.

So disturbances continued and mile after mile of homesteads and rice-fields were deserted. Then in June 1885 the first British Collector was appointed to Jelebu, and in September 1886 the territorial and tribal chiefs signed a treaty surrendering administration to the British officer of whose continued assistance they asked to be assured. In 1887 another of the Nine Counties, Rembau, applied for a British officer with the stipulation that one-third of the revenue should be paid to the chiefs; the huge increase of revenue due to rubber led a quarter of a century later to a modification of that stipulation, the chiefs agreeing that they should draw fixed allowances, and the balance of the third be devoted to Malay welfare.

In 1889 the rulers of Rembau and Tampin joined a number of little Counties adjacent to Sri Menanti to form a Negri Sembilan, Gemencheh, hitherto unknown to fame, being added to make up the number. There was now one British Resident for the Nine Counties and another for Sungai Ujong and Jelebu. In 1895 the whole of what is now Negri Sembilan elected Tengku Antah Yang di-pertuan of the entire country and accepted one Resident. Perhaps the example of more than two centuries of peace under the Dutch and English at Malacca and direct dealings with the English there made the Malays of Selangor and Negri Sembilan readier than Perak to welcome British protection—in spite of the Naning war. But the tact of early officials must not be underrated.

As for Pahang, the first British official to visit it was Frank Swettenham, who had done so well in Selangor. In 1885 he was sent there to try to settle a boundary dispute and a quarrel between the ruler and his brother. This he did, and at the same time warned the Sultan of the financial improvidence of granting large concessions of land. In the light of his own experience in Selangor he recommended the appointment of an Agent of the Straits Settlements to live at Pekan, watch the interests of British subjects and make himself acceptable to the Malays. (Sir) Hugh Clifford was sent to try to arrange for a treaty, which, with the help of the very able Dato' Mantri of Johore, he contrived to do. The important point was Pahang's acceptance of a British Agent with functions similar to those of a Consular Officer. The Agent found himself in an environment mediaeval and chaotic. The revenue system was organized merely to put money into the coffers of the ruler and his chiefs. Even onions and curry-stuffs were taxed exorbitantly, and the Sultan granted monopolies for the sale of household articles and farmed out the collection of import duties on nearly every commodity. Gold ore had to be sold to His Highness' agents at about half its market price. Huge concessions of land were made to Europeans and Chinese who had greased the palms of royal favourites, the Sultan not caring if the land belonged to his chiefs or was already being mined by Chinese or Malays.

As soon as it was rumoured that the British would protect the State, the hunt for concessions became keener than ever, concessions bound to retard development and narrow sources of revenue. The Sultan's favourites imposed heavy fines for mediaeval offences, carrying off wives and daughters in default of payment and killing any who resisted. When the Agent, Hugh Clifford, tried to tackle this maladministration of justice, to draft laws and define jurisdiction, the Sultan added a clause to the draft providing penalties for the harbouring of fugitive slaves, and the chiefs interfered with the new judges. A Malay was convicted of abetting the breach of a monopoly and fined $32 or six months' cash earnings, because his wife made oil for her own use out of four coconuts.

When Clifford went on a visit to Singapore, two women were tortured and two Sakai boys ducked and beaten (so severely that one died) on suspicion of stealing the gold ring of a creese. Then in February 1888 a British Chinese subject, Go Hin, was stabbed in the precincts of the palace, where none would dare to lift a hand without royal orders. Rumour said the Sultan coveted the victim's wife. The Malay Chief Justice offered a reward for information as to the incident, whether the stabbing was due to man, djinn or devil. The Chinese died. The Governor came up from Singapore and required the Sultan to accept a British Resident. Advised by the Sultan of Johore to comply, the Sultan of Pahang did so, hoping that no more would be said about the murder of Go Hin and that Her Majesty Queen Victoria would be satisfied with his expression of regret.

The problems that faced the first Resident were the abolition of slavery, the regulation of forced labour, the fixing of allowances for the Sultan and chiefs in place of feudal dues, and the framing of laws for the tenure of land. The fixing of allowances, however careful, was bound to cause discontent. Actually the list was drawn up by an untrustworthy Malay who inserted the names of his friends and omitted those of his enemies; it was passed by the Regent, the Sultan's heir, because he thought that the Resident had approved it, and though it was criticized by the Sultan, His Highness forgot to revise it. At a meeting of the State Council the Resident accepted some alterations, but pointed out that the allowances amounted to two-thirds of the State revenue. A chief, with aboriginal blood and a reputation as a fighter, the Orang Kaya Pahlawan of Semantan, had his seal of office withdrawn by the Sultan for refusing to obey the orders of government, as in days before British protection he had once refused to obey the orders of the Sultan not to collect taxes. He incited his people to disobey all government regulations until he should get the allowance of a major chief. When he thought the government planned to arrest him, he ambushed a Collector's boat and captured a police-station, after which his followers rose from a hundred to 600 men. The Sultan took the field against the rebel, and much impressed the Resident by his transport and commissariat arrangements as well as by his skill in guerilla warfare. But the rebels vanished into the jungle, thence from time to time raiding unprotected stations. Some of the chiefs urged the Sultan to expel the British, and the Dato' Maharaja Purba of Jelai got ready to attack Kuala Lipis. Some accounts relate that the Sultan connived at the proposals; if so, His Highness soon changed his mind. The Sultan increased his forces to 1000 men, and there were now 240 Sikh troops. But To' Gajah, another chief, joined forces with the Semantan rebel, and together they fled into Kelantan. The Sultan and the Maharaja Purba visited the Governor at Singapore, where the latter voiced his grievances, inadequate allowances for himself and his headmen, the threat to his mining land by a grant given to a British company, and his people's dislike of the new regulations for forced labour, even though they were to be paid as they never had been before. An amnesty was proclaimed for all rebels except the two leaders, who were, however, promised their lives if they surrendered. But a holy fanatic of Trengganu foretold their invulnerability and victory. They collected a hundred men and raided Kuala Tembeling. The Dato' Maharaja Purba and Sikhs from Perak and Selangor and the Colony put the rebels to flight. Hugh Clifford pursued the rebels and their few followers into Kelantan and Trengganu, which were still under Siam. Siamese commissioners accompanied him. But with the connivance of the Sultan of Trengganu the rebels escaped. In November 1895 the Orang Kaya Pahlawan and five followers surrendered to the Siamese. To' Gajah was reported to have died in Trengganu. This last of Malay risings had dragged on four years from December 1891. Few lives were lost in the fighting, although many of the rebels' followers must have died of privation in the jungle.

In 1902 the desire of Sir Frank Swettenham to extend British protection over the northern Malay States had led Lord Curzon to consider him "a swashbuckler of the most truculent type". But in 1904 the Entente Cordiale with France removed the fear of 30 years that a forward policy in the north of Malaya would lead France to grab Siam and exclude British commerce. And in 1909 the desire to build a railway connecting Bangkok with the Malayan system led to Siam transferring to the protection of Great Britain Kedah, Perlis, Kelantan and Trengganu, four States that had never brought her any revenue. The secret convention of 1897 which required Siam to get British sanction even for the grant of a prospecting licence to any European over land in the Malay peninsula was abrogated. Britain agreed to the abolition of extra-territorial rights over her subjects in Siam. And Britain gave Siam a loan of £4 million at 4 per cent interest for the construction of her railway. Kedah paid a Penang lawyer to protest against the disposal of states as if they were merchandise, and a relic of this token objection survived in a clause in the treaty made between Kedah and Great Britain stipulating that Kedah should never be joined to the Straits Settlements or to any other Malay State without the approval of the Sultan-in-Council.

Kedah and Perlis were too near Penang not to have felt some at least of the influences of the present century. But as Rupert Emerson, an American critic of British ways, has remarked, there should linger "no romantic notion", that "in Kelantan and Trengganu the British or even the Siamese intervention disrupted a somewhat primitive but idyllic government". In Trengganu, when the British entered, "all manner of crime was rampant, the peasantry was mercilessly downtrodden, but the land was full of holy men, and the cries of the miserable were drowned in the noise of ostentatious prayer". In Kelantan, when Siam appointed a British Adviser in 1903, the Raja and his uncles had the monopoly of a mint that smelted tin into coin the most trumpery in any part of the world. What revenue there was, was paid to clerks in the palace to be borne off on elephants to a *cache* in the hills that served as a royal bank. Salaries were paid only when the clerks happened to have cash in hand. This mediaeval mess it was not very difficult to clear up. The legacy of misrule that retarded the progress of Kelantan for 30 years was a concession to a police inspector, Duff, who had accompanied Clifford into Kelantan in pursuit of the Pahang rebels. In return for payment to the Raja of £2000 and 2000 shares, Duff had been given 3000 square miles, or one-third of Kelantan, together with wide seignorial powers and other privileges. The purchase of these rights by Kelantan led to prolonged costly and notorious litigation and a claim by the Duff Company for £1,091,269. It is too long a story for these pages, but the concession saddled Kelantan with debt for years.

The last Malay state to seek British protection was Johore. Freed after 1641 from attacks by Acheh and Portugal, this relic of the Malacca Sultanate had held sway over Malaya from Perak downwards, over the Riau archipelago and over Sumatran fiefs valuable for trade in pepper and gold. In 1699 Sultan Mahmud, last of the Malacca royal house and a mad pervert, was murdered at Kota Tinggi and was succeeded by his prime minister the Bendahara, whereupon a Minangkabau pretender, Raja Kechil, attacked and ruled for four years until ousted by Bugis whose help Johore had invoked once before in a war with Jambi. From 1772 Bugis underkings became the real rulers at Riau, from where by war and diplomacy they dominated the west coast of Malaya, until Sulaiman, son of the first Bendahara Sultan, at last sought the assistance of the Dutch, surrendering to them Rembau and Linggi and granting monopolies. In 1782 the most famous Bugis warrior, Raja Haji, quarrelling with the Dutch was killed in an attack on Malacca. Thereafter, in spite of some resistance by the Bugis and later by the Malays, the Dutch governed at Riau until 1795 when the English occupied Malacca and handed authority back to Sultan Mahmud (d.1812),

BRITAIN AND THE MALAY STATES 77

whose son Husain (p. 59) was to sell them Singapore. In the nineteenth century Johore had become in many respects highly civilized. In 1882 Maharaja Abu-Bakar entertained Prince Albert Victor and Prince (later King) George. The princes described "the huge drawing-room of the palace like one of the state-rooms at Windsor and furnished from London". In the afternoon the Maharaja drove a four-in-hand to Singapore races, with Prince George beside him on the box. In 1885 a treaty was signed by which Great Britain promised Johore protection against external attack, and formally recognized the Ruler's change of style from Maharaja to Sultan. Johore, on its part, was not to enter into any engagement with any foreign state or to make any grant or concession to other than British subjects or persons of the Chinese, Malay or *other Oriental* race. Johore also agreed to accept a British Consular Agent if ever it were desired to appoint one. But by 1914 the development of the rubber industry had turned Johore into an important state beyond the experience and ability of its Malay administration to manage; the Sultan, therefore, signed a treaty accepting a General Adviser "whose advice must be asked for and acted upon on all matters affecting the general administration of the country and on all questions other than those touching Malay religion and custom".

Except for Patani all the Malay States of the peninsula had accepted British protection and advice. To ensure that protection force such as in civilized territory would have been exercised by the police had with the co-operation of the more enlightened Malay chiefs been employed in Negri Sembilan and Pahang. Only in Perak the tactless eagerness of the first Resident had led to events that called for military intervention, with which even the more friendly chiefs could hardly show sympathy.

After 1945 all the Malay States, together with Penang and Malacca, formed the Federation of Malaya, which on 31 August, 1957, became independent.

CHAPTER IX

BRITISH ADMINISTRATION

i. In the Straits Settlements

When in 1786 the East India Company rented the island of Penang from the Sultan of Kedah, there were few inhabitants and no local Malay administration for it to supplant or reform. This was fortunate, because being interested only in commerce the Directors so handled matters that its administration became a notorious failure. Within three years the total value of Penang's imports and exports rose to $853,592, within eight years to double that sum. Yet the Settlement never paid its way. Its founder and first Superintendent, Francis Light, was instructed not to levy taxes and was given no staff to do so. Until 1800 the revenue was derived from lump sums paid by Chinese for spirit, opium and gambling farms, the only course possible in the absence of customs officials. But in one year Penang was paid only $72,000 for farms out of which the Chinese bidder made a profit of $186,000, while in the same year Singapore with less than a quarter of Penang's population got $75,000 for its farms. Light had no training in administration. To attract a population, he let Asiatics occupy what land they could clear under promise of a title in the future. Europeans, including servants of the Company, were given large areas, and Light and his business partner, a second cousin of Sir Walter Scott, appropriated the best sites. When death and migration brought valuable lands on the market, the government had no funds for their purchase, and they were bought by Scott's firm, which also engaged in usury and acquired land by foreclosing on mortgages and buying from impoverished debtors or the representatives of absent or dead owners. Grants had been promised with no condition that failure to cultivate would, after a term of years, involve resumption. There was no land revenue and no prospect of getting it. The Company even had to rent land from Scott as a site for Government House. In

1805 Penang still had "few roads and public buildings, no medical service, no department for the collection of revenue, the scantiest provision for the maintenance of law and order, and strangely enough no law". Then the Directors attempted reform. No official was to engage in trade. No land was to be alienated to Europeans without the Directors' approval and in all titles there was to be a clause for increasing quit-rent with increase in cultivation. But Trafalgar scotched the idea of a naval arsenal, and lack of local timber killed it and ship-building for a China trade. Absence of European demand for its spices, civil war in Acheh, Siamese aggression and anarchy in the Malay States, competition first with the British and then with the Dutch in Java and later with Singapore, these success-ive and various misfortunes marred Penang's trade and in 1832 the seat of government was transferred to Raffles' Lion City.

1824, the year that saw Singapore ceded to Great Britain by the Malays, saw also the cession of Malacca by Holland. But the British had held Malacca from 1795 till 1818, and its administration was in the obsolescent tradition of Penang rather than on the progressive lines of Raffles' Singapore. The East India Company was faced with two problems at Malacca, namely land and Naning, and its civilians mishandled both. Large areas were in the hands of Dutch landlords who had the right to let their property in return for a tithe of its produce payable to themselves or their nominees. These nominees were Chinese, who bought the right of collecting rents and squeezed the Malay tenants, whom they regarded as barbarians. Under this mediaeval Malay system the government still owned the soil, but there was no stipulation that land would be resumed if it were not cultivated, and no machinery for a just assessment of tithes. The rapacity of the Chinese middleman discouraged agriculture. So, commerce having passed to Penang, the government bought out the landlords' rights for annual pensions that came to less than £2000, in the hope of deriving revenue from improvement in agriculture. But while retaining the old mediaeval system of tenure for land that was cultivated, it decided that after 1830 titles should be issued for other land in accordance with English law. There were no surveyors, and hopeless confusion arose as to what land was held under the old system and what under the new. The Recorder pronounced the new land rules illegal. The Malays demurred to paying cash in lieu of the tithe. The Land Office failed to defray its expenses plus the landlords' pensions. The problem was not settled till the '80s, when a Governor from New Zealand, Sir Frederick Weld, introduced a system under which all dealings with land have to be registered in a government office.

The Naning war falls within the province of general history rather than the province of administration. But it is worthy of note that the civilians of the East India Company discovered in their archives the actual relations between the Dutch at Malacca and Naning only after they had stirred up an unjust war that cost £100,000 and resulted in subduing a district whose revenue in 1833 was $762! Naturally it was years before the British ventured on extension of territory in Malaya.

Singapore, too, narrowly escaped administration on the bad old lines. Farquhar, its first Resident, held the traditional views about raising revenue from gambling and cock-fighting, and, worse still, he owned slaves. As for Raffles, he did not hesitate to avail himself of the Company's permission to hold land, and he instructed Farquhar to reserve half the lots on the sea-front at Singapore for himself, his relatives and friends. Moreover, like all other of the Company's servants, Raffles was a jack-of-all-trades. To a friend he wrote: "I have had everything to new-mould from first to last; to introduce a system of energy, purity and encouragement." That was his forte, but he had the more concrete tasks of making laws for his new city. He drafted regulations for a land registry, port rules, police regulations, laws forbidding gaming, cock-fighting and the slave trade. "All this work," as he wrote home, is "a pleasant duty enough in England where you have books, hard heads and lawyers to refer to, but here by no means easy, where all must depend on my own judgment and foresight." At law Raffles was an amateur, and legal chaos continued to prevail. Raffles' greatest financial measure was to declare Singapore a port whose "trade was open to ships and vessels of every nation free of duty, equally and alike to all". But this measure was very much more than financial. It was ethical reform in the interests of the Asiatic, so long cabined and confined by monopolies. On that score it stands beside Raffles' abolition of slavery. Even then Raffles was not satisfied. He wanted not only to free the Asiatic and his trade but to do something for his advancement. With this last aim he established an "Institution, having for its object the cultivation of the languages of China, Siam and the Malayan archipelago, and the improvement of the moral and intellectual conditions of the inhabitants of those countries". In education, as in law, Raffles was an amateur, and he failed to recognize that education must work upwards from the elementary school. But he was the pioneer of the idea that a colonial government must study the welfare of the people.

One swallow does not make a spring, and men with the enthusiasm and ideals of Raffles were rare in the Malaya of those days. No Bengal civilian studied Malay or Chinese or wanted to be transferred to Settlements made up of three ports with no field for promotion. With empire thrust upon it, the Company had little experience of the art of government and had yet to realize the need for lawyers and engineers in distant parts of the world or the need for its own good to study local interests. In an effort to make the Straits Settlements pay their way, the Company from time to time threatened the free trade that was the life-blood of the Malayan ports. For after 1833 the Government of India lost its monopoly of trade with China, and the Indian Treasury had every year to meet a heavy deficit in the Straits budget. The Company did its best for three distant ports without prospects, with hinterland unopened and with Dutch competition all around them. Often it lacked information and it lacked imagination. When it passed an act to force the rupee on a dollar country, the people of the Straits Settlements were ready for a transfer to the Crown.

The year after the Indian Mutiny the East India Company was abolished as an anachronism and for nine uneventful years the Straits Settlements were under the control of the India Office, until in 1867 Great Britain bowed to local demand to put them under the Colonial Office. Not yet had Indian patriots arisen to talk of Greater India and include ancient Singapura in the ambit of their thoughts.

Under the East India Company and the India Office there had been no local representation. As a Crown Colony, the Settlements came to have unofficial members not only on their Legislative Council but on the Executive Council. The preponderance of Chinese in the population led to a preponderance of Chinese members, who ranked next to the British members in number. But Eurasians and Malays and Indians were also appointed. Except for two British members of the Legislative Council chosen by the Chambers of Commerce, all these unofficials were nominated by the Governor. In a community largely foreign popular election was impracticable. In a community so composite, an official majority, though hardly ever used, was the ultimate means for holding the balance between conflicting interests. Before they were sundered in 1945 and Singapore was left a solitary Colony by itself, the Straits Settlements, outliving piracy and Chinese riots, reached a height of prosperity beyond the dreams even of Raffles.

ii. In the Malay States

When Malay States first accepted British protection, bureaucracy was superimposed in Negri Sembilan on a democracy that gave votes to women and protected the rights of the humblest. The change would have been a matter for regret except that this matriarchal democracy of Minangkabau colonists suffered from one flaw, which it never contrived to mend: it insisted that the election of all its representatives, from the Ruler down to the humblest tribal elder, must be unanimous. What was the result? In the 1830's there were five claimants and in 1874, when the British intervened, two claimants to the throne, with the four territorial chiefs, the electors, each asserting the paramount claim of his own favourite and maintaining his view by force of spear and creese. The office of Ruler or Yang di-pertuan, or, as it is abbreviated, Yam-tuan, was in fact a foreign and Hindu excrescence, which the Minangkabau tribal system never absorbed or before the days of British tutelage tried to absorb. For though the Yam-tuan had, like other Malay rulers, the divine right of one whose ancestors had been the incarnation of Hindu gods, and who himself was the shadow of Allah upon earth, yet compared with the rulers of the patriarchal Malay States he had no authority. He could levy no taxes except fees for cock-fights. For his maintenance he lived on land inherited from the tribal wife of the founder of his house and he was given traditional petty presents at his installation and on the occasion of marriages and other feasts. He was supreme arbiter and judge, if the territorial chiefs chose to invite him to adjudicate, which they never did. He was Caliph or head of the Muslim theocracy in any territory where the local chief did not arrogate the title for himself—and he always did. The Yam-tuan should have been first in a State Council, as other rulers were, but no council ever met. For, like the Ruler, the four territorial chiefs or Undang were, in a Minangkabau polity, excrescences inherited from the patriarchal overlordship of the fifteenth-century Sultans of Malacca: older excrescences than the Yam-tuan and more powerful, as they had got absorbed by accepting uterine descent and conforming to matriarchal custom. Since the days when d'Albuquerque took Malacca, the Undang had been leaderless, or rather their overlords the Sultans of Johore, who represented the Malacca line, had been fugitives, far away and powerless, so that the Undang regarded themselves as petty kings and never collaborated except when the threat of Bugis domination led them to create the first Yam-tuan in the eighteenth century.

Below the Undang are the Lembagas, the real chiefs of the matrilineal Minangkabau tribes. They also had to be elected unanimously, and in old days there were often indecent delays over their obsequies and fights at the graveside, a new chief having to be appointed before his predecessor was buried. If the electors failed to reach unanimity, the choice came to be made by the territorial chief in council with the other tribal chiefs within his borders. But even that council sometimes failed to agree. And it was left for the British to arrange final appeal to a State Council of the four Undang under the chairmanship of the Yam-tuan. Once appointed, the Lembaga was, and is, an invaluable official. Under Malay rule he marked the boundaries of tribal lands, settled the transmission of property on death or divorce, had jurisdiction in cases of lesser crime, torts and debts, kept an eye open for the misdeeds of territorial chiefs and had an official to spy on the conduct of his subordinates, the elders, as his Undang also had one to spy on his. While legal powers have passed now into the hands of British and Malay magistrates and land officers, the Lembaga has remained their trusted expert adviser on all matters of tribal land.

The Lembaga's subordinates are elders (*buapa*) elected by members of sub-tribes. In old-world sayings the Lembaga is described as a hawk, but the elder irreverently as a chattering mynah, whose province is not tribal land but the disputatious tribal folk male and female. He is the witness for all formal payments made to or by a member of his sub-tribe, and for the declaration of a husband's private property at marriage and at its return on divorce. Before the advent of the British he also had minimal jurisdiction.

On the whole the Minangkabau democracy of Negri Sembilan has accepted accretions whether Malay or British with equanimity, confident in its power to bring even the British official under its "sceptre of fascination". But its matrilineal democrats never really sought to remedy the two fundamental weaknesses of their constitution. They were so intent on the principle of unanimity that they never realized the advantage of accepting a majority vote, so that before the British period minorities were always creating civil strife. They were so suspicious of tyranny that they never gave the Yam-tuan the power required to federalize their territory. The Undang or four territorial chiefs never met in council under the Yam-tuan, as each of them met in council with his own tribal chiefs. The British creation of a Council with the Yam-tuan as chairman, the four Undang as members and a majority vote cemented the warring elements of the little State of Negri Sembilan for the first time in history.

Theorists will point out how the study of his law and constitution has made the Malay of Negri Sembilan perhaps the most intelligent in the peninsula, and will complain that bureaucracy has overlaid a healthy indigenous polity. But openly and covertly that democracy has contrived to function. There are still all the old Malay offices, their holders elected still in the old fashion. One evidence of their power is the almost total absence of Malay litigants from courts constituted by the British with British and Malay magistrates. Only when the law demands attendance at a government office, as for example when dealings in land have to be registered, do the female democrats, in whose names ancestral holdings are held, flock with their tribal chief before the collector and expound and demand their tribal rights with dominant persistence.

If some explanation of the benefits of British administration in Negri Sembilan is required, civil wars, barbarous punishments and exorbitant taxation afford indisputable excuse for our belated interference in the other states.

At the head of every one of these patriarchal states is a ruler, Yang di-pertuan—"He who is made lord", to employ the Malay style, the Raja in the parlance of his Hindu ancestors, or Sultan to use the term preferred by his latest faith. Like the Chinese of the Chou period 3000 years ago, the primitive Malay had credited his chiefs with magic powers under the influence perhaps of Babylonian ideas. Even as late as 1874 a Perak audience saw nothing fantastic in their Sultan acting as a medium at a shaman's *séance* and prophesying the death of the first British Resident—whose murder he intended to compass. With the advent of the Hindu period the Malay ruler had become an incarnation of a god, most often of Indra, controller of weather and lord of Mount Meru, the Hindu Olympus, with its 33 gods. The myth has a measure of practical interest still because the astrological notions centring round the Hindu Meru have affected and left their impress on the political structure of the Malay States. Like Burma, Siam and Cambodia, mediaeval Malacca and most of the modern states have constitutions founded on the astrological numbers 4, 8, 16 and 32. In all those countries there were 4 chief ministers and 4 chief consorts for the king. In most Malay countries there are not only 4 chief ministers, but 8 major chiefs and 16 minor chiefs, and, below the last, mediaeval Malacca and modern Perak have had also 32 petty chiefs. Thirty-two chiefs plus a king made up the number of gods in Indra's heaven, and a Malay kingdom was conceived as "an image of the heavenly world of stars and gods". Its *roi soleil* was associated with all that was bright. Only the king could fly a white flag or wear yellow garments. As the king of Siam claimed any white elephants, so the ruler of Negri Sembilan took as his perquisites albino birds, albino animals and albino children.

Coming down to earth, a Malay ruler had certain recognized powers as well as many prerogatives. Only he could pardon a traitor, a murderer and the abductor of a married woman. In theory at least he was a constitutional monarch. Tomé Pires tells us how in old Malacca death sentences were reviewed by the Sultan, the prime minister, the admiral and the chief of police; and treaties between the Sultan of Perak and the Dutch, for example, were signed by the Ruler and major chiefs.

In mediaeval Malacca all the chiefs except the 32 bore the title of Mantri; and every Mantri had judicial powers and the duty of collecting tribute, which was paid by adjacent subject states in tin or gold. The Bendahara or Prime Minister had powers of life and death not only in his own domain but anywhere in the state in the absence of the Sultan. The Temenggong, or chief of police, had everywhere the same duties, namely to arrest criminals, build prisons and carry out executions; he superintended forts and moats and supervised markets and weights and measures. A Sultan had a chamberlain, secretary and treasurer, styled Penghulu Bendahari, who kept a roster of royal slaves and collected the Ruler's personal revenue. The Shahbandars or port officers and collectors of customs dues are said by Pires to have been of several nationalities. There were governors of tributary districts with the title of Mandalika.

The prime task of chiefs in mediaeval Malacca was to prosecute an imperialist policy for the glory of the royal house and for the advancement of trade that brought wealth to rajas and chiefs. As for domestic policy, except Johore and Kedah in the present century, no independent Malay states expended money on roads, medicine, education or any of the scientific branches of a civilized government. Instead of a standing army there were mercenaries and swashbucklers attached to the court or to chiefs' households. The only civil servants were tax-collectors and police, who were also the myrmidons of the chiefs.

The obligations of any power concerned with the protection of Malaya's brawling and lawless states were clear. Great

Britain had to ensure peace and order and to build up communications that would consolidate isolated districts into homogeneous states. It had to contrive that rulers in theory constitutional should be so in practice. It had to enlarge the government to represent the rights and interests of immigrants who according to Muslim mediaeval theory had as pagans no rights at all. It had to arrange for public revenues to be spent for public welfare. It had to transfer administration from the hands of interested amateurs to the hands of disinterested specialists and to increase the branches of government to include such modern subjects as medicine and agriculture and engineering.

As soon as the Malay chiefs had been allotted compensation for the loss of hereditary privileges in the shape of fixed allowances, it did not take long to win their co-operation, and the old order quickly gave way to the new. The change was greatly facilitated by the two main principles of Malay rule: the consultation of their chiefs by the rulers and the virtual conduct of government by the Bendahara or Prime Minister. Just as a Sultan of Malacca had delegated authority to his Bendahara, so now the Sultans were content to entrust administration to the Residents. For the kernel of the treaty with every state was that, while all revenue should be collected and all appointments made in the name of the Ruler, he should accept a British Resident whose advice had to be invited and followed upon all matters other than those touching Malay religion and custom. But how were these British Residents to discover the wishes of the Malays and to explain to them the objects of British policy? The Indian Mutiny had revealed the folly of legislating for Asiatics without means of ascertaining whether laws of foreign origin were objectionable to them or not. So, following the model of the Indian Councils Act of 1861 and mindful of the Sultans' time-honoured councils, the British instituted State Councils with executive and legislative powers. The President of every Council was the Ruler, and leading chiefs were members, but there was the radical innovation that the British Resident and Chinese merchants (and later other British officials and unofficials and Indians) were also members. Taxation, land laws, the review of death sentences, the enforced carrying of torches by night to reduce robberies, the firing on a crowd of Chinese rioters, the construction of a railway, compulsory vaccination, trespass by buffaloes, the preservation of wild guttapercha trees, an application for permission to trap elephants, the efficacy of a rat-poison for rice-fields, the abolition of slavery—the topics broached at early meetings of these State Councils were a strange mixture. So, too, was the personnel of the new civil service in those days. A few officials from the neighbouring colony were available like (Sir) William Maxwell and (Sir) Frank Swettenham, who did yeoman work and made for themselves distinguished careers. But the most able and tactful of the Residents, Sir Hugh Low, had been a botanist. One upcountry district officer had been a midshipman and won great popularity among the Malays by holding cock-fights to settle disputes, the owner of the winning bird having the suit given in his favour. Another was an Italian who kept a Malay smith and was elated when he got a hawker to palm off one of his smith's creeses on the Resident as a genuine antique. But already by the late '90's of the last century cadets were recruited for the Malay States and soon there was formed a united Malayan Civil Service, its members liable to be stationed in the Straits Settlements or the Malay States, honours men from British Universities, who sat for the competitive examinations prescribed for the Home and Indian Civil Services. Later the same type was recruited, though theoretically they were members of a service common to all the Colonies, and they were appointed no longer after competitive examination but by nomination.

Although the Residents were responsible to the Governor of the Straits Settlements, lack of communications and of any federal link led to tiresome differences in the taxation and legislation of the four protected states. Each passed its own laws and its own annual budget and each had its own state officers. So in 1895 Perak, Selangor, Negri Sembilan and Pahang were federalized under a Resident-General. From the time when Francis Light negotiated the acquisition of Penang down to the MacMichael treaties of 1945 there was a tendency for the British Government to assume that when the attainment of a good end is in question the end justifies the means, and though pains had been taken to institute State Councils, the signature of the Rulers was accepted on this treaty of federation without their prior consultation with those bodies:—even in Malay times the most arbitrary Sultan had at least made a pretence of consulting his chiefs, and since 1889 laws had been enacted by the Ruler in Council. Nothing in the new treaty was to curtail the powers of rulers in their several states, though they were now set the acrobatic task of following the advice of a Resident, of a Resident-General and occasionally of the Governor also. Under it the wealthier states were to be persuaded to take the unprecedented but admirable step of promising to give the poorer such assistance in money and officials as the Resident-General might advise. A durbar of the Rulers was constituted, a sort of federal council in embryo, though it was without legislative or financial powers. And there was nothing in the nature of an executive council to limit the authority of the Resident-General.

Rubber coming on the top of tin gave an impetus to the development of the federal constitution. For when Sultan Idris was led by the Resident of Perak to issue a circular exhorting his subjects to take up the easy job of squatting in the shade and tapping rubber-trees, Malays accepted this reflection on their industry in good part, but having often been bitten over novel crops waited to see the result of European and Chinese planting. But the tin mines and rubber plantations that those foreigners opened in every state rapidly grew into great industries, which for financial confidence demanded representation; so in 1909 the first High Commissioner got approval for a Federal Council that eviscerated the four State Councils, leaving only petty and local matters on their agenda. On the new Federal Council the Rulers became ordinary members with no power of veto and with the disadvantage that their rank prevented them from joining in debate; besides, they were in the anomalous "position of advising themselves and that only as individual members of a majority or a minority as the case might be". The President of the Federal Council was the High Commissioner (who was also Governor of the adjacent Colony), and other members were the Resident-General, the four Residents and four unofficials. of whom three were British and one Chinese. In 1913 the Legal

Adviser and another unofficial were added, and in 1920 the Treasurer and yet another official. Before the reform of the Council by Sir Lawrence Guillemard (1920–27) the unofficials had been raised to eight, of whom five were Europeans, two Chinese and one a Malay chief.

In 1927 the Rulers signed an agreement for the reconstitution of the Federal Council, with thirteen officials and eleven unofficials. The new officials were heads of large departments, appointed so that they could explain policy and answer criticisms. Of the unofficials four were to be Malays, taking the place of the Rulers, who to their great satisfaction now gave up their seats. Although consulted outside the federal chamber, Their Highnesses had for years sat and listened in silence to what everyone regarded as the allocation of state revenue by the federal executive authority and unofficials interested in tin and rubber. But there was so much money that the Rulers felt no inclination to criticize. Nor were they disposed to challenge emergency legislation passed without prior reference to them during the First World War. Then two events opened their eyes to the realization that their states were in theory federated, but in practice amalgamated.

The first event that made Malays eye federation critically was the refusal of the five states, Johore, Kedah, Kelantan, Trengganu and Perlis, that came under British protection in 1909, to enter it on any terms. The treaty with Kedah went so far as to stipulate that it should never be joined to the Colony or to any other Malay state without the consent of its State Council. The treaties with Johore and Kedah stipulated that Malay and European officials should be on a footing of equality. Johore had voluntarily asked for protection as the modern government of a growing population was outside its experience, so that it had reason to expect consideration. But even "the right to administer the four northern States which Great Britain possessed" on taking over suzerainty from Siam "was exchanged by her for the right to advise, and she thus conferred a degree of internal independence which is an indulgence in a suzerain power". The newly protected states enjoyed privileges beyond the dreams of the federated, notably financial autonomy. And the people of the Federated Malay States were aware that it was their revenues that had financed the loan to Siam which had bought the British suzerainty over the four northern states. The Rulers of the Federated Malay States felt that they had hardly had a square deal.

The second event was the depression after the war of 1914, which led to charges against the federal authorities of extravagance at the expense of the constituent states. The expenditure of millions of dollars on unprofitable sections of the railway and on the futile construction of a railway dock in the drifting silt of Prai excited general criticism. Why had no one (except the Sultan of Johore) foreseen the imminent competition of the motor-car and the motor lorry? Critics shut their eyes to the many public works and services that were due to federation.

In spite of all, even Malays had become conscious that federation had widened the horizon of the state with benefit to the peasant, who for centuries had lived (as Malays say) like a frog under a coconut shell. But now (1933) Downing Street performed a *volte-face* characteristic of its Malayan policy and approved of decentralization. After 1909 the Resident-General had been called Chief Secretary, to emphasize his subordination to the High Commissioner, but his powers had remained unchanged; now his place was taken by a Federal Secretary, too junior in rank to the Residents to be an autocrat. Laws were no longer to be passed by the Federal Council, but by the four State Councils again. History is likely to smile over this ostrich-like gesture. But decentralization appeared no laughing-matter to the heads of such departments as dealt with agriculture, education, medicine and public works, who since 1927 had been members of the Federal Council and whose unchallenged fiat had run throughout the Colony and the Federation. Now they saw their departments disintegrating and their fiats challenged by state heads of departments, their own subordinates. Their fears were exaggerated, but they looked with envy at the unified departments that were left intact, the police, the customs, the survey and the labour departments and military defence. Responsibility for the public debt remained with the Federal Council: without its sanction no State could raise a loan. The broom of impetuous reform halted at the threshold of the treasury.

With its great revenues Malaya had been able to afford the service of such competent specialists that no constitutional change was likely to put back the clock of progress. Malaya's forests were threaded by a thousand miles of railway and five thousand miles of metalled roads. The fifth of the country that was cultivated had been surveyed from trigonometrical data. There was scientific conservation of the small supply of hard timber in Malaya's boundless forests. Agriculturists had increased the rice crops and done much to improve copra and the quality of pineapples and the fruits. Only the Fisheries Department remained inadequately staffed and equipped until after the Japanese war.

But the weak spot under any scheme for decentralization was the State Councils. In Johore and Kedah these were efficient bodies with Malays accustomed to the ways of Singapore and Penang and having a good notion of modern government. But under the shadow of the Federal Council no State Council in the four oldest protected states had grown to maturity. The members were the Sultans, the Resident, some Malay chiefs, occasionally one or two British officials and unofficials and one or two Chinese. Proceedings were in Malay and the views of the Sultan were practically always those of the Resident and the views of the chiefs those of the Sultan. It was the old Eastern story: "What are legions and motor-cars thundering by? What spikenard? What bezoar compared to the twinkle of a royal eye-lash?" To qualify these effete councils to deal with larger issues European and Indian unofficials were now made members, as also were younger Malays with a modern education and modern minds. All unofficial members of the Federal Council were to have served first on these State Councils. And to ensure federal uniformity without obtrusiveness the two federal officers responsible for finance and legislation were appointed members of all the State Councils! Nine sets of individual laws were now enacted by nine legislative bodies in a country the size of England. It was farcical make-believe and it failed in its object; the five States outside the Federation still showed no inclination to come in. Why should they? Without cost to themselves they enjoyed a pattern for their laws in federal legislation and borrowed officials who had been trained in administration, tropical medicine, agriculture and so on at the expense of the Colony and the Federated Malay States. Not that the Unfederated States were now averse from paying their quota. They grudged no expense to preserve their autonomy. For, as a former High Commissioner, Sir Lawrence Guillemard (1920–27), wrote when he started decentralization in the Federation, in the other States "the British Advisers had to deal with a different type of ruler from the type of the '70's and they set about their task in a different way. They have never attempted to be anything except Advisers", and guided the Unfederated States "along lines in no wise bureaucratic and for the benefit primarily of the Malays". Though wealth was in the hands of Chinese and Europeans, there was no doubt as to which was the favoured race in an Unfederated State before the Japanese invasion.

The difference between the Malay States that came first under our protection and a state like Johore in 1914 is well illustrated by the written constitution that was drafted by English lawyers for Johore's first Sultan, Abubakar, in 1895. That constitution with one amendment made in 1912 has remained in force and was taken as a pattern by the Malays for the constitution of all protected states. Under the original constitution there were to be a Council of Ministers and a Council of State. The ministers, who were the assistants and advisers of the Ruler, had to be Malays professing the Muhammadan faith. Before the treaty of 1914 the members of the Council of State had to be Johore subjects, though not necessarily Malays or Muslims, but after 1914 membership was thrown open, as in all the states, to British officials and others not required to be Johore subjects or to take an oath of allegiance to the Sultan. The Council of Ministers had neither executive nor legislative powers; the main function of the Council of State is legislative. By an amendment to the constitution in 1912 a third or Executive Council was created on the model of similar councils in British colonies, its province including routine matters of administration, the initiation of legislation, advice to the Ruler on death sentences, applications for all but small holdings of agricultural land and for all mining rights, all contracts and tenders for public works. To every General Adviser the session of this last Council was the most helpful and interesting official function of the week, especially as the chair was nearly always taken by Sultan Ibrahim, with his vivid personality, his intimate knowledge of his country and the shrewd brain characteristic of his house. The administration of Johore was carried on by a Malay Mantri or Prime Minister with a Malay State Secretary as the channel for all communications to and from the Government.

In Kedah, Kelantan and Trengganu there were State Councils combining executive and legislative functions on the model of those in the Federated States. In Kedah a State Council was established as far back as 1905 under Siamese pressure, but membership except for the admission of the British Adviser was limited to Malays. In all the states transferred by Siam, the civil service, even in its higher ranks, was staffed mainly by Malays, while the clerical service, which in the Federated States is full of Chinese and Indians, was restricted to local Malays.

In all the Malay States the higher ranks of the technical departments were until 1957 staffed almost entirely by European engineers, surveyors, foresters, doctors, agriculturists and educationists. But in Kelantan and Trengganu the small revenue kept these technical services backward.

After 1914, when Johore accepted British advice, Malaya had three types of constitution:

(1) The Straits Settlements (that is, the island of Singapore, the island of Penang, along with Province Wellesley, and the territory of Malacca, including Naning) were a British Colony.

(2) Perak, Selangor, Negri Sembilan and Pahang had been protectorates since the '70's and '80's of the last century, and after 1895 were the Federated Malay States.

(3) Kedah, Perlis, Kelantan and Trengganu, transferred to Great Britain by Siam in 1909, and Johore, which asked for a British General Adviser in 1914, were separate protected states, described as the Unfederated Malay States.

After the defeat of Japan, Malaya was divided into two divisions only:

(*a*) the Colony of Singapore

and

(*b*) a Union of all the Malay States plus the Settlements of Penang (along with Province Wellesley) and of Malacca (along with Naning). In 1932 the Dindings were given back to Perak.

In 1948 the Union was changed into a Federation of Malaya.

In February 1955 the British Government having already promised that the continuance of Communist terrorism should not delay political progress agreed at a conference in London that full self-government and independence within the Commonwealth should be proclaimed if possible by August, 1957. During the interim before that proclamation internal defence and security were to be in charge of a Malayan Minister and external defence and relations in the hands of the British High Commissioner. It was decided further that British Advisers to the several States should be withdrawn. From 31 August, 1957, the Federation of Malaya became independent.

CHAPTER X

THE REIGN OF LAW

IN NO sphere was British influence more beneficent than in the sphere of law. But British was not the first European influence experienced in one Malay port: Malacca had been under the reign of both Portuguese and Dutch law. The Portuguese appointed leading citizens as magistrates with civil and criminal jurisdiction, and from their decision appeal lay to a Chief Justice; but there was no divorce between the judiciary and the executive, because in criminal cases triable in his court the Chief Justice had to apply for the advice and confirmation of the Governor. To adjudicate in the disputes of the Minangkabaus of Naning and to punish their misdeeds, a Portuguese was appointed bailiff for life, but he too had administrative functions. The Bendahara appointed by the Portuguese to have jurisdiction over foreign Asiatics in Malacca derived part of his income from fines. Portuguese justice, indeed, was no less corrupt than Portuguese administration, and it was the Portuguese from whom words for "rack", "torture" and "dungeon" crept into the Malay language. Then, when in 1641 Malacca was wrested from Portugal by the Dutch, the Malays came under a people with a profound respect for law, but it was still law that adjudged the ferocious punishments of the age. When the crew of a Dutch patrol ship butchered the crew and passengers of a Moorish ship off Kedah in revolting circumstances, the Netherlands East India Company with even-handed justice sentenced the offenders to lose their right hands and be broken on a cross before execution. Keel-hauling was regarded as a mild punishment for the Company's servants. And slaves were liable to inhuman floggings. Such had been the law of the conqueror before the British period, and it was a happy accident of history that by the time the British came to impose a uniform system of criminal law throughout the Malay peninsula, law, or, as Hobbes called it, "the public conscience", was coloured with the humane ideas that had followed the French

THE REIGN OF LAW 97

Revolution. When Lord Minto burnt the stocks and the racks and released the debtors from the Dutch prison at Malacca, it was no idle gesture but the symbol of a new era.

Yet when the British had rented the island of Penang for their first settlement, a trading company was very slow to introduce a proper legal system. Although within three years the population of that island had risen to 10,000, Francis Light, its first Superintendent, was told vaguely to preserve order by inflicting imprisonment or other common punishments. By 1792 he had to arrange for the Asiatic headmen to exercise jurisdiction in the case of offences committed by persons of their own race; for it was not till near Light's death of malaria in 1794 that a regular magistrate was appointed to meet the needs of an expanding population. Cases of murder by other than British subjects were tried by courts-martial, consisting of not less than five members chosen from officers of the army and from respectable citizens. For the trial of British subjects there was no provision at all. When in 1800 instructions for the administration of justice were at last issued, they prescribed that the law for Penang was to be "the law of the different peoples and tribes of which the inhabitants consist, tempered by such parts of the British law as are of universal application". It is hardly surprising that when the first Judge arrived, he concluded there was no law except the law of nature. In two cases where he applied the Statute of Frauds, he was overruled by the Lieutenant-Governor. It was not until 1807, or twenty years after its foundation, that Penang got a proper legal system.

In Singapore Raffles took the line that "the old and irrational in the societies with which he dealt must be rooted out that they might be replaced by the universal and natural law of nature, the outstanding embodiment of which was undoubtedly the British Common Law". To the Government of India he reported that "we cannot do better than apply the general principles of British law to all, equally and alike, without distinction of tribe or nation, under such modifications only as local circumstances and peculiarities and a due consideration for the weakness and prejudices of the native part of the population, may from time to time suggest. . . . Something like a code, which shall explain in a few words what is considered a

D

crime and what is the punishment attached to it, seems indispensable." But until 1826 legal chaos prevailed, the Resident administering Chinese and Malay law, and having no power over Europeans.

The introduction of a satisfactory legal system into the Straits Settlements took time. It was not till after 1867, when the Settlements came under the Colonial Office that a Supreme Court was established and the executive ceased to have judicial functions. The Indian Penal and Criminal Procedure Codes were adopted with few alterations. There was also a Civil Procedure Code. And a Civil Law Ordinance "introduced the English law relating to partnership, corporations, banks and banking, principal and agents, carriers by land and sea, marine insurance, life and fire insurance and mercantile law generally". Not only was a Court of Appeal instituted, but appeals could be made in appropriate cases to the Privy Council. Magistrates in the Colony before the Japanese war might be British, Malay, Chinese or Eurasian.

Except that there could be only British and Malay magistrates and that two assessors took the place of juries, the judicial system of the Straits Settlements was the model for that of the Malay States. And to assess the value of this importation of British law into those states, some knowledge of the Malay systems is necessary.

Universal validity, impartiality and comparative humanity distinguish British justice, and only one Malay system of law can challenge any comparison. That is the primitive Indonesian system of which Hindu and Muslim law had left only relics in the patriarchal States, but which was in full force in Negri Sembilan seventy years ago and is still the civil law of Minangkabau colonists. Put its customary provisions alongside the despotic rule and brutal hybrid law of the patriarchal Malay States and at once it is apparent why this matrilineal law commands the passionate regard of the Minangkabaus as a Magna Charta, or, as they express it, "a couch for the sleeper, a shelter for the wayfarer, a ship for the navigator, a heritage for the farmer". No Raja ever dared to tamper with its validity and no Muslim Kathi to challenge its unorthodox principles. It was safe in the keeping of a democracy of inland agriculturists impervious to foreign influences. Every peasant can quote the sayings that embody it and the clever have compiled innumerable digests with the impossible aim of identifying the law of exogamous clans with the Muslim canon.

Life in a clan is communal, and the Hindu sword of execution, the Hindu tortures and prison cage, and the Hindu and Muslim lopping off of thieving hands would have involved the loss of workers on tribal fields. So except for heinous and incorrigible offenders tribal penalties always took the form of restitution, a fowl or goat for assault, a man from the slayer's tribe in the event of homicide. With a rigidity unavoidable in law designed for a large population British law sentences murderers to death and cares nothing for tribal loss or for compensation in the shape of fowls, goats and sisters' sons. It refuses to accept the Minangkabau view that arson, robbery, swindling and marriage with a woman of one's own tribe are capital offences. When accident is proved, it will not convict of homicide, and what the Minangkabau custom condemns as criminal cheating it often relegates to a civil court. In all these points the Indian Penal Code introduced by the British was an advance on Indonesian criminal law.

But with Minangkabau civil law neither Muslim nor British law interfered. The law of property remains matrilineal. In theory ancestral property still belongs to the tribe and in practice descends to daughters and granddaughters or sisters and nieces and so on. This tribal law had two great advantages in former days. To prevent the loss of a pair of hands a tribe would defray a tribesman's debt rather than let him be lost to it as the debt-slave of a creditor. Secondly, it safeguarded—and still safeguards—the proprietary rights of wives, divorcees and widows, giving a divorcee, for example, a half share of all property acquired jointly during married life. In modern times this tribal law has had another beneficial result. It has kept land from passing into the hands of foreign moneylenders for the liquidation of individual debts.

A primitive fairness to women was the one redeeming feature in the law of the patriarchal Malay States. Villagers on the Perak River, for example, still insist that on divorce half the land acquired during wedlock shall be given to an unfaithful wife, if she has helped to cultivate it, and one-third if she has not. A proposal by the Perak State Council to apply the general principle of Muhammadan law which gives a man a share double that of a woman has found no acceptance. For years Malay headmen were allowed to give evidence explaining these anomalies of local customary law. Then in 1927 the British Supreme Court ruled that this oral evidence on the law of a state was inadmissible. But how then was any court or land office to discover what was the Malay law? An enactment was passed enabling points to be stated for the decision of the Ruler-in-Council, a decision that unfortunately is likely to follow Muslim jurisprudence rather than earlier custom. Another danger now threatens the customary rights of Malay women, and that is the possibility of the construction of Malay law within the new Federation following the strict Muslim law of Penang and Malacca. The Muslims of those two Settlements would be shocked not only at the customary rights of women, but at the customary evasion of the Muslim ban on the taking of interest. A Malay creditor will accept a charge on land, allowing him to enjoy the profits or part of the profits of the crop, such profits not to be placed against the money owed but to be in lieu of interest, until the debt is repaid in full. Here the peasant has preferred the practice of old Hindu days to compliance with the commandments of his latest faith.

Criminal law in the patriarchal states was a tissue of barbarities, inconsistencies and class favouritism, three of the most damning flaws in the administration of justice. Evolved for the mixed population of mediaeval ports like Malacca, Kedah and Pahang, it was introduced mainly by Indians, at first Hindu and later Muslim. And our knowledge of it is due to five digests, a Malacca digest *ca.* A.D. 1450, a Pahang digest of 1596, a Kedah digest of port laws dated 1650, an eighteenth-century digest entitled the Ninety-nine Laws of Perak, and a Johore digest of 1789 which is largely based on that of Malacca. Tomé Pires tells us that in mediaeval Malacca a man might be impaled or burnt alive or beaten on the chest to death according to the nature of his crime. The Pahang digest prescribes for a traitor three hundred and sixty tortures, to be followed by quartering. In 1880 one could have seen a Pahang youth guilty of *lèse-*

majesté by some palace intrigue with his scalp down over his eyes and his body tied to a stake to be drowned by the rising tide. His accomplice would be the victim of obscene tortures or of execution by drowning. Alternative to the death penalty in Malacca of the fifteenth century were such punishments as scalping or cutting out the tongue of a betrayer of royal commands. The last Sultan of Malacca is alleged to have had his Lord High Admiral castrated for bringing false charges that led to the execution of a Prime Minister. The veracity of a witness was tested in those days by the Indo-Chinese methods of ordeal by diving or by plunging a hand into boiling water or molten tin, to extract a potsherd that as a concession to Islam bore an inscription calling on Allah and the Four Archangels to reveal which party spoke the truth. The Hindu generalization in the Malacca digest as to the death sentence for ten offences mirrors the contemporary disregard for human life. Even a slave who had been struck a blow could lawfully kill his assailant within three days, and if he killed him later was merely fined, though, as the compiler of the digest remarks, Muslim law would hold him guilty of murder. But the Malacca and the Pahang digests exhibit inconsistencies that may have been purposely inserted to leave a Sultan scope to apply customary Hindu or Muslim law as prejudice or policy dictated. Yet a Sultan ruled by the consent of his subjects, apathetic and superstitious though they might be, and the adoption of Hindu law with its condonation of murder or payment of blood-money made no insurmountable break with the Malay custom of substituting a fine for the death sentence, a custom obviously welcomed for the sake of their purse by Perak's Sayid justiciars of the eighteenth century; Perak's Ninety-nine laws let a murderer pay a fine and provide a buffalo or white goat for the funeral feast. Whereas the usual penalty for theft was the loss of a hand on the first and second occasion and the loss of a foot for the third or fourth offences, these Perak Sayids allowed a thief to compound for a first offence, to lose a finger for a second and to be banished for a third. In fact, so discrepant are the provisions of the several digests that there was little meaning in a statement made in the Perak State Council in 1878 that Malay law was for the most part "unwritten though generally understood and appearing to differ little from the codes of law formerly in force in Malay States". Even the law of torts dealing mainly with damage by buffaloes to crops was not uniform throughout the peninsula.

When the British started to administer the Malay States, the outmoded cruelty of Muslim criminal law and the impracticability of the Muslim law of evidence, along with its contradiction of the Malay acceptance of circumstantial evidence, made the Malay rulers glad to follow in the footsteps of Turkey and Egypt and to adopt the Indian Penal Code and a law of evidence that was a compromise between two systems they could not reconcile. In this matter the Malays saw the desirability of interference with their religion and custom.

CHAPTER XI

TRADE, MONOPOLIZED AND FREE,
AND FINANCE

i

STATEMENTS by early Chinese voyagers have been taken to imply that Indian traders visited the Malay world in neolithic times before the Aryan invasion of India. Certainly they must have needled the way there for the coming of Hindu priests and Buddhist monks and for the Hindu adventurers who founded little port kingdoms on Malaya's estuaries. As we have seen, desire for the gold and spices of the lands beyond the Ganges greatly increased the amount of Indian shipping at the opening of the Christian era. Buddhism had lessened Hindu prejudice against crossing the sea and mixing with barbarians. Larger Indian ships were being built and the monsoon winds were understood. But in spite of bigger ships, or rather because of them, Indian traders naturally shunned the calms of the Malacca Straits by crossing on foot the narrow Malay peninsula on their way to Indo-China. Others were content to go no farther than the west coast of Malaya. And the beads dug up at Kuala Selinsing in the north of Perak and the Indian and Roman beads from Kota Tinggi on the Johore River suggest that international trade started with neolithic Indonesians as primitive as the naked Sakai or the Dayak, who both deck their persons with those ornaments. Among primitive Malays it must have been the practice for chiefs to take the lead in commercial transactions as the Sakai headman and the Batak raja still do. The practice was not only natural but inevitable in communities where property belonged not to the individual but to the tribe. And when Indian adventurers married the daughters of Malay headmen, the practice was fortified by the growth of families not only bilingual but possessed of the quicker intelligence desirable for transacting business with the foreign customer. Under such conditions it was easy enough for the Hindus to introduce the Indian system of royal trading. I-tsing, the Buddhist monk who travelled at the end of the seventh century, tells how the king of Sri Vijaya possessed ships that sailed with cargoes to and from India. So it is in a literal sense that Arabs trading in the ninth century with Kedah declare that the Maharaja of Sri Vijaya was made as rich as any king in the Indies by trade in cloves, sandalwood and nutmegs, in ivory, ebony and gold, in camphor from Sumatra and tin from Malaya. To this royal commerce the coming of Islam made no difference. Tomé Pires records how at Malacca Muzaffar Shah "bought and built junks and sent them out with merchants" and how the ruler of Malacca waxed rich by "putting his share in every junk that goes out". He also relates how by ships from the Malay archipelago and the Far East "dues are not paid on merchandise, but only presents to the king and his ministers". Even on the visits of the early rulers of Malacca to China there is a caustic but illuminating remark made by a Chinese chronicler, that the barbarians brought tribute not from any sense of duty but in quest of the advantages of trade.

To mediaeval Malacca resorted merchants from Cairo, Arabia, Turkey, Armenia, Byzantium, Persia, India, Burma, Siam, Cambodia, Champa, China and the Malay archipelago as far away as Celebes. The merchandise exchanged at this *entrepôt* half-way between India and China was such Malayan produce as tin, cloves, nutmegs, mace, pepper, musk, camphor, benzoin, sandalwood, honey, wax and slaves; gold from Pahang, Sumatra, Java, Brunei and Cochin China; tapestries, incense and seeds for dyeing from Arabia; cloths from Pulicat and Cambay; Chinese silks and brocades and porcelain; silver from Burma, Siam and China; rosewater, opium, pearls, quicksilver, saltpetre, copperware and ironware; gilded coffers from Canton and birds of paradise to set in Turkish and Arabian turbans. It is to be noted that it is precisely the most valuable of this merchandise—gold, silks, ivory and sandalwood—that were the perquisites of Malaya's merchant kings down to the British period. In mediaeval Malacca chiefs as well as Sultans traded. The *Malay Annals* say that the Bendahara or Prime Minister to Malacca's last Sultan never failed in his ventures and was richer than the richest Tamil in the port. Pires talks of the

Bendahara's great jewels and his five quintals of gold, but Pires also records that Sultan Mansur Shah died possessed of 120 quintals of gold besides quantities of precious stones.

In the seventeenth century, as Dutch records show, the Sultans of Kedah traded with India, taking cargoes of tin and elephants to Bengal and Coromandel in their own royal vessels. It was with the rulers of Kedah and Johore that the Dutch monopolists made so many ineffectual agreements for the purchase of all the tin from their countries, and there is frequent mention of vessels belonging to the Sultans and their chiefs. Early in the eighteenth century there was a Sultan's brother at Riau who nearly caused a rebellion by "engrossing all trade in his own hands, buying and selling at his own prices". And Bugis traders, for whose merchant vessels a Sultan of Malacca had special laws drawn up, soon blossomed into chiefs who not only married into the Malay ruling families but usurped their commerce. As late as the nineteenth century the old prerogatives were asserted. For in the middle of that century the Singapore Chamber of Commerce was complaining that the Temenggong of Johore monopolized trade in Malaya's indigenous gutta-percha, his armed followers intercepting cargoes for Singapore and securing nearly all a crop in which there was then a boom: "it was inferred that extreme influence of some kind was used, or some part of it would have found its way to parties who offered much higher prices".

This Malay tradition of royal trading brought two most evil consequences. In the first place, protected by sumptuary laws, the royal merchants prevented the emergence of a commercial middle class. In the second place, when the arrival of the Portuguese and Dutch monopolists put an end to intercourse between Indian merchant princes and Malay ruling families, the one chance for Malays to get to understand the uses of capital was extinguished, the royal families becoming more and more Malay with no fresh Indian blood to keep alive commercial instincts. Undoubtedly European monopolists hampered Malay enterprise and damaged Malay trade. But even after 1511 Asian commerce flourished. In 1622 Dutch shipping in the Malay archipelago was 24,000 tons and Asian 81,000 tons. Then in the seventeenth and eighteenth centuries the commerce of

Perak, Kedah and Johore was ruined by Achehnese attacks: Acheh even destroyed Kedah's pepper plantations so as to have a monopoly of the pepper trade. When Penang was founded by the British in 1786 and free trade established in Malaya for the first time, Malay commerce revived. But when the steamship arrived, then it decayed everywhere. Apart from Bugis vessels that till the advent of steamships sailed from and to Celebes with the monsoons, Malay shipping had had no chance to develop under the surveillance of the patrol boats of the Dutch and Acheh. Malay commercial ties with Java and Sumatra and Coromandel and Bengal had been damaged by the Portuguese and the Dutch. The Malay peasant, it is true, became richer in the British period and soon learnt to spend, but no one taught him how to invest, and his religion frowned on the taking of interest. So he stood naked to the winds of commerce that blew from China, India and Europe. Chinese and Indians not only had shipping of their own, while the Malay, a better sailor, had practically none, but Chinese and Indians had commercial connections between their countries of origin and the Peninsula of their adoption. And as the *pax Britannica* increased the tide of immigration, so the plight of the Malays grew worse, though for a few decades the boom in rubber hooded their eyes. Neither Chinese nor Indian will admit the Malay into their firms, and now that the Malay is perturbed and anxious to enter commerce, he finds that the Chinese and Indian have preceded him even in British firms and have taken care to keep alive the tradition that the Malay is lazy. A Malay once tried to start dealing in rice in a state predominantly Malay, but as the only motor transport was owned by Chinese, they gave their own race preferential rates for lorries in the hope of squeezing out the interloper. A Malay co-operative society arranged to sell its rubber direct to a British firm in Singapore, but as this was a blow at the Chinese middleman the firm's large Chinese clientèle threatened to withdraw their custom unless the arrangement was cancelled. In his own country the Malay is boycotted as a trader by implacable foreigners. Examples are innumerable (p. 143). The trade of Malaya is in the clutch especially of the Chinese, to whom compromise over business is unthinkable. In Burma the

TRADE, MONOPOLIZED AND FREE 107

government has discriminated against firms that have neglected to employ Burmese.

It was free trade, introduced at the founding of Penang in 1786, that attracted Chinese and Indian settlers. It and the eclipse of the Dutch during the Napoleonic wars led to the rapid development of Penang that yet never fulfilled its early promise. Chosen as a place for refitting ships, it proved unsuitable for docks, as the opposite coast was also to prove. Lying at the extreme periphery of the Malay archipelago, Penang was central only for trade with Burma and Siamese Malaya and with northern Sumatra, which as late as 1824 produced—a legacy from Acheh's greater days—almost 60 per cent of the world's pepper. Hardly, however, was it founded when China took Indian opium instead of pepper and tin for her tea. Not only was Penang at the edge of the Malayan map, but pirates made the long sail up the calm Straits of Malacca so hazardous a venture that Riau remained the chief port of resort for the Bugis, and local boats still preferred the nearer port of Malacca.

Not that the ancient harbour of Malacca could fulfil modern needs. Policy and geography had directed much of its trade to Penang. Its harbour was too shallow for the increasing draught of shipping. The anarchic condition of the Malay States hampered even Malacca's local trade. And finally the founding of Singapore reduced it to a depot for its last and greatest rival.

The commerce of the two lesser ports had its ups and downs. By 1865 (long before the days of rubber) the trade of Malacca was six times as big as in 1829. The trade of Penang in those days depended largely on the price of Sumatran pepper, though it also had important Chinese customers interested in its seaslugs, birds' nests and sharks' fins. But before the days of rubber the ratio between the trade of the three Settlements was fairly constant, Singapore enjoying about three-quarters of it. And though there have long been no pirates to deter shipping from Penang, Singapore will always be pre-eminent by reason of its central position and its great landlocked harbour.

Singapore, however, did not come to be numbered among the ten greatest ports in the world without setbacks. The

D**

British occupation of Hongkong in 1842 temporarily deprived it of much traffic. The French conquest of Indo-China made Saigon and Haiphong its competitors. The establishment of Dutch shipping lines between Holland and Netherlands India and between the islands of the archipelago took away a large part of local commerce. The Malay States opened Port Swettenham for direct transport of tin and rubber and of the commodities needed for those two great industries. Finally, in 1933, in order to halt the menace of cheap Japanese textiles and other wares, Netherlands India had to impose preferential tariffs on foreign imports. But for all these losses the demand of the world's motor industry for tin and rubber and the economic advance of Siam more than compensated. In 1830 the total trade of the Straits Settlements was just under £5 million; in 1890 Malaya's trade was over £32 million; by 1900 that total had more than doubled; by 1910 it was £80 million odd and by 1920 it was over £237½ million. In 1926 it was to soar to £264 million, exceeding the trade of all other British Colonies combined. Even in 1938, when Malaya's trade had dropped to £121½ million, or less than half its peak figure, it still exceeded the total trade of New Zealand, or the combined trade of Britain's seventeen African Colonies and was more than half the trade of British India. Singapore's three miles of wharves were strewn with crates and baskets containing all the wares of Asia, Europe and America; rickshas from Canton; motor-cars from Cowley, Detroit and Milan; cotton cloths from Manchester, Java, Pulicat and Japan; petroleum from Sarawak, Dutch Borneo and Sumatra; tea, silk, porcelain and blackwood furniture from China; silks, cycles and electric fittings from Japan; piece goods, books, tobacco and machinery from Britain; watches and clocks from Switzerland; matches from Britain, Sweden and Japan; Austrian bentwood chairs; Austrian breakfast services with cups reduced to fit the local egg; shoes from Nottingham; frocks and cosmetics from Paris. One-third of Malaya's imports were foodstuffs for her abnormal immigrant population: rice from Rangoon and Saigon; fresh fruit from Java; pickled vegetables from China; tinned fruits and jams from Britain and New Zealand; cold-storage meat and fruit from Australia; tea from India; beer from Germany; whiskey from Scotland; rice-spirit from China; bottled red fish from Macassar; caviare from Russia. From the same wharves rubber, palm-oil, copra, pineapples, tin, iron ore, gold, tungsten ore, bauxite, manganese and ilmenite, as well as salted and dried fish, sharks' fins and sea-slugs, pepper, rattans and other immemorial produce of the Malay jungle, were put aboard to be carried to all the markets of the world. Of those markets none has been more important than New York. In 1955 the United States bought approximately one-fifth of the rubber exported from Malaya and nearly three-fifths of the tin.

In the economic field Great Britain conferred no greater boon upon Malaya than this: that after centuries of monopoly by kings and conquerors she allowed its people to sell all the produce of mine, forest and estate in free markets at competitive prices, making no attempt to control the price or flow of exports for her own interest. If it be objected that the modern form of monopoly is restriction of the output of tin and rubber, the answer is that when there is restriction it is imposed as much for the benefit of the labourer and smallholder as for the benefit of capitalist and government, and it may even preserve production for the benefit of the consumer.

ii

Let us turn from the ledgers of the merchant to the ledgers of the Malayan governments.

At the close of the nineteenth century there was little disparity between the annual revenue of the three Straits Settlements and that of the four Federated Malay States; for neither did it amount to £1 million. Then para-rubber reached the tapping stage and for more than forty years the Colony was the poor relation of the Protectorate, even excluding the new Unfederated States. When Penang and Malacca formed part of a federation with all the Malay states, Singapore was left the fragment of a colony whose mean annual revenue for five years before the Japanese occupation was just over £4 million and the island had heavy commitments on public buildings and docks. To add to its difficulties the sale of opium, which once produced nearly half the revenue of the three Settlements and in 1937 almost a quarter, had been abolished throughout the British Commonwealth. Against that occurrence an Opium Reserve Replacement Fund was started for the three Straits Settlements and in 1955 under the name of Special Reserve amounted for Singapore to £11½ million. In addition there was a Singapore Development Reserve of £3⅜ million. After opium the next largest item of its revenue had always come from import duties on tobacco, liquor and petroleum, and this item produced over £8 million a year, income-tax bringing in about the same sum. These two sources produced two-thirds of the total revenue which for 1955 was £24,278,588⅛, the surplus over expenditure being £1,050,054. The public debt of the island was small. And its General Reserve (over and above the Special Reserve) amounted at the end of 1955 to £16⅛ million, a large part of it immobilized in the shape of long-term loans to the Singapore Improvement Trust and the Federation of Malaya.

The largest revenue ever enjoyed by the four Federated Malay States was just over £12½ million in 1927, and their lowest was just over £5 million in 1932. These violent fluctuations were due entirely to the rise and fall in the world's demand for tin and rubber, particularly in the demand from the United States of America. The end of the First World War found the Federation a country of arrears in such services as education, agriculture and forestry. But the development of estates continued to demand further large expenditure on communications, and in 1921–2 a loan of $80 million was raised for this purpose. In 1930 nearly £900,000, or 9·2 per cent of the Federation's total expenditure, was spent on medical and anti-malarial measures, and £471,621, or 5 per cent of the same expenditure, on education. Four years later, consequent on the great depression, these votes were almost halved and there were drastic economies in every department.

The revenue of all the Malay States, Federated and Unfederated, in 1937 was just about £13⅝ million, to which the Federation contributed just under £9½ million and Johore just under £2½ million, the largest revenue in its history. 1937 found Johore with no public debts and a surplus of more than £5

TRADE, MONOPOLIZED AND FREE   111

million and Kedah with no debt and a surplus of £900,000. Of all the Malay States only Kelantan and Trengganu were indebted, and their debt was to the Colony and the Federation. The Unfederated States for years enjoyed the services of government officials of all departments administrative and technical without having to pay for their training or defray any part of their salaries. With increasing revenues they agreed to pay a proportionate share. In 1955 the revenue of the new Federation of all the Malay States, Penang and Malacca amounted approximately to £93 million. But in 1954 the International Bank Mission had found the revenue only enough to cover current expenditure at its level then, including that due to the Communist emergency.

iii

Malaya's wealth had permitted a contribution of more than £3 a head of her population to the war effort or more than all other British colonies and protectorates together. In 1949 and 1950 the sale of tin brought more than ninety million U.S.A. dollars to the Empire dollar pool each year. For the period 1947–51 the Malayan governments derived £35 million from export duty on rubber. In 1950 the Malayan output (694,086 tons) was 37½ per cent of the world's natural rubber, though, so far from profiteering, those who had invested some £70 million in rubber (and ploughed back 25 per cent out of their earnings) got on an average only about 3 per cent on their money.

Before the Japanese war Singapore was the world's fifth greatest port but now ranks probably third behind London and New York. In 1950 Malaya's exports were valued at £461 million and her imports at £337 million, and her dollar earnings equalled £125 million. The great fall in 1952 emphasized her dependence on two major products. In 1956 Pan-Malayan exports were valued at a little more than £486 million and imports at £484½ millions. Dollar earnings were £68½ million.

CHAPTER XII

INDUSTRIES, PAST AND PRESENT

MAN's oldest industries are concerned with the getting of food. The pigmy Negritos, Malaya's most primitive people today, live on jungle fruits and roots and game. The races who passed through the Peninsula eight thousand years ago left the bones of the wild beasts whose flesh they ate in the caves and rock-shelters of the northern states and the debris of the molluscs that formed the diet of some of them in the shell-heaps of Province Wellesley. Not till we come to that higher type, the Sakai (or Senoi) Indonesian hillmen, do we encounter agricultural methods that illustrate how the primitive Malay passed from shifting to permanent cultivation. Some Sakai move every year or so to plant fresh clearings with rice, millet, yams, tapioca, maize and vegetables; others live in the same clearing for a decade or longer, cutting down the trees and scrub on adjacent slopes in rotation. This was the stage the civilized Malay had experienced and passed many centuries ago. But some modern Malays still practised shifting cultivation, until the British forbade a practice so wasteful of timber. It was not that the Malays were ignorant of irrigation. But there were, what has hardly been recognized, two types of Malay in the peninsula: the landsman of the Kedah and Kelantan plains and of Negri Sembilan, and the coastal people whose ancestors were sea-gipsies and exploited forest as they exploited river and sea. The coastal Malay, like the Orang Laut or sea-tribes of today, was a fisherman originally and a pirate when international commerce offered a richer sea harvest, and the sea-gipsies, who were the earliest settlers in Malaya and the Riau archipelago, turned to shifting cultivation for what rice they wanted and took no more interest in agriculture than is taken by their descendants who dive for coins at the Tanjong Pagar docks. So the polyglot merchants who made Malacca a port kingdom had to import their rice from Sumatra and Java. For even in 1512 the only neighbouring places mentioned by Tomé Pires as having enough rice for their needs are Bruas and Muar. The solitary rice-patch in some narrow valley against a background of dark forest or green orchards is a delight to the eye, but if it escape drought, it is still too liable to the depredations of pig, rats and deer, not to speak of the dreaded elephant, to command the labour and care of any intelligent Malay with other scope. So until Malacca was founded about 1400, southern Malaya remained sparsely populated, though in the north some of the fertile plains may have been irrigated under the kings of Langkasuka, the hinduized little state which Chinese chroniclers date back to the first century A.D. Possibly Kedah Kelantan and Patani must have planted wet rice under the sovereignty of Sri Vijaya, and when that Malay Buddhist empire and its colonies fell before Hindu Majapahit in the fourteenth century, northern Malaya came first under the influence of the Javanese and then under that of the Th'ai, or modern Siamese, both of them expert in the irrigation of rice-fields. It is for these historical reasons that rice-planting reached so high a standard in the north, where wide irrigable plains attracted a population large enough for rice to be cultivated even on a commercial scale. Before the sporadic immigration of small bodies of Javanese and Banjarese in modern times, the only other expert rice-planters in Malaya were the Minangkabau colonists of Negri Sembilan. A century ago Kedah and Minangkabau states behind Malacca grew enough rice to be able to export their surplus to the nearest ports. Kelantan and Patani must have produced more than enough for their own needs and Perak's crop was adequate for its small population. But before the days of roads and railways, drought or pests often meant an insufficient diet of maize or tapioca for the people of remote isolated hamlets. From 1919 to 1921, when a famine in India led to restriction on the export of rice from India, the Malayan governments spent £4,900,000 on buying rice from other countries.

To open $7\frac{1}{2}$ acres of irrigated rice-field cost in 1948 about $360. In 1913 it was reckoned that with rice at $2\frac{1}{4}$d. a *gantang* (about $6\frac{2}{3}$ lb.) the owner of $2\frac{1}{2}$ acres got next to nothing the first year and then about £5 a year. The cost of planting and preparing the fields is made up mainly of the owner's labour, and that has risen in value with the rise in the cost of living. Rice just before the war cost one shilling a *gantang*, so that a crop from 2½ acres was then worth £26 a year. But the cash yield is deceptive. Such a holding, it has been calculated, will provide rice for a family of six with a surplus to sell. Moreover, to produce a crop of rice the planter has to work for only five months in the year.

Writing in 1884 Sir William Maxwell calculated that a square mile of irrigated fields in Province Wellesley should support 1936 souls, which is well below the ratio of 36 per cent of all the rice consumed in Malaya, that was produced in 1939 from some 700,000 acres. By 1955 the Federation produced 420,000 tons of rice against 367,000 tons imported.

Work on a rice-field occupies less than half the year. But the Malay is always a handyman rather than a specialist, so that the rice-planter has other sources of food and income. Chinese writers in 1416 noted how the Malacca holdings were then full, as they are today, of sugarcane, bananas, fruit-trees, vegetables, gourds and melons. Many Malay fruit-trees have been imported from abroad, mangoes from India, the sapodilla guava and papaya by the Portuguese from South America. Tomé Pires tells how in every street of mediaeval Malacca there were women who sold fruit and other produce and some had stalls in front of their houses. On his trip up the east coast in 1830 Munshi Abdullah saw markets held from sunset to dark by women who carried their garden stuffs to the town in head-baskets. The Malacca stalls and the Kelantan markets may have been due to the example of Javanese from Majapahit. Under British encouragement such markets were revived in some districts, but, like rice, most garden stuffs are bought for a low price by the ubiquitous Chinese shopkeeper, to whom the Malay villagers are generally in debt.

Apart from rice, two only of the Malay's crops can be counted important, namely copra and para-rubber. Coconut palms, though indigenous to Malayan shores, were few in the south, when the British first entered the Malay States. Outside Malacca and Negri Sembilan the population was sparse and cultivation scanty. Often palms had been felled in hostile raids. The Johore Malays felled 7620 coconut palms to make Dutch earthworks at the siege of Malacca in 1641. Several times

INDUSTRIES, PAST AND PRESENT 115

Dutch punitive forces from Malacca burnt Minangkabau villages in Naning and Rembau, destroying rice-fields and orchards. The Minangkabaus retaliated in similar fashion on Malacca territory. At the beginning of the last century, when Siam invaded Kedah, 20,000 Malays left their homesteads to flee into British territory. War inland and piracy along the coasts so disheartened the Malay villager that at first the British experienced difficulty in persuading him to plant coconut palms beyond his family's needs. Even when he had planted them, for lack of simple means of making copra he would sell the nuts to the Chinese middleman at an uneconomic price. But before the fall of Malaya many Malays had been taught by the British experts of the Agricultural Department to make their own copra and they formed the bulk of the 300,000 Asiatic smallholders, whose coconut plantations were valued at £15 million. The revenue from copra and coconut oil in 1956 was nearly £7 million.

Tin was for centuries the greatest asset of Malaya. Then in 1877 an expedition under Mr. (later Sir) Henry Wickham brought 70,000 seeds of para-rubber out of Brazil and started Asia's rubber industry with 22 seedlings despatched from Kew to the Botanic Gardens at Singapore. In 1905 Malaya still contributed only 200 tons to the world's market against 62,000 tons of wild rubber from South America and Africa. But the motor industry had begun and by 1910 Brazilian speculators were able to force the price up to 12s. a lb. The boom excited London as cargoes of spices had excited it in the days of Elizabeth. A barber in the Strand discovered a customer to be a Malayan planter in whose estates his savings were invested, and he refused to take a penny from an alchemist who had transmuted his copper into gold. By shaking this modern pagoda-tree an office-boy in the City won a windfall of several hundred pounds. New companies were floated. Mincing Lane hourly mangled euphonious Malay place-names. Malays cut down their orchards and planted up even their rice-swamps with rubber. By 1914 there was more plantation than wild rubber. By 1920 Malaya exported 196,000 tons, or 53 per cent of the world's production. Then the world slump caused supply to exceed demand, and, the price of rubber falling to 6d. a lb., many estates were faced with bankruptcy. The Dutch, considering it impossible and impolitic to control the output of Malay holdings in Sumatra, refused to join in any scheme for restriction. But from 1922 till 1928 the British restricted the export from Malaya and Ceylon to 60 per cent of the potential output with a view to stabilizing the price at 1*s*. 3*d*. a lb. This measure saved many companies from ruin, giving them time to effect economies, but it failed in the end. The reason for this failure was that consumers were encouraged to reclaim used rubber, and the Dutch companies and Sumatran Malays planted an area more than three times as large as the rubber acreage when restriction began. In 1928 restriction was abandoned and the industry turned for its salvation to the science it had neglected. Vast sums, for example, had been wasted on clean weeding that led to erosion of soil and inferior trees. Now the British planter followed the Dutch in selecting high-yielding strains and in bud-grafting, which more than doubles the flow of latex with a consequent reduction in the cost of tapping. But in 1930 the price of rubber fell to 6*d*. a lb. and in 1932 to just over 2*d*. From June 1934 until the outbreak of war all the British colonies and protectorates concerned together with Netherlands India, Indo-China and Siam were under agreement to restrict, the basic quotas for 1934 being 504,000 tons for Malaya and 352,000 tons for Netherlands India. Consumers, American and British, as well as planters, were interested in the survival of estates and in a stable price for their produce, and all took part in the administration of the scheme. Malaya's governments got their revenue for social services from an export duty on rubber and from import duties on the commodities required for rubber companies and their 350,000 coolies and for the Asiatic planter. Above all, hundreds of thousands of Asiatics depended on the survival of the industry for a livelihood. The League of Nations blessed restriction for improving the economic conditions in many tropical countries and for advancing international trade.

In 1937 the value of the rubber Malaya exported (of which one-third came from adjacent countries) was just over £56½ million, or nearly half Malaya's total trade, and in 1956 it was just over £255½ million. At the beginning of 1957 the external capital invested in Malaya's rubber industry was £64 million. And of more than 3½ million acres planted with rubber 46 per cent belonged to Asiatic estates and smallholdings. From 1956 to meet the menace of synthetic rubber perfected during the war the government agreed to subsidize the replanting of estates with high-yielding clones.

Before the days of para-rubber many other commercial crops had been tried. Early in the fifteenth century Chinese voyagers reported the manufacture of sago in Malacca. Judging from its Malay name the pineapple was introduced in the Portuguese period, perhaps by fifteenth-century Filipino settlers, and Malaya now produces 90 per cent of Great Britain's tinned pine. As early as the same period the Minangkabaus of the hinterland were famous for the export of betel. Barbosa, writing in 1516, records how in Kedah "is grown much pepper, very good and fine, which is conveyed to Malacca and thence to China", but to preserve their monopoly Achinese invaders destroyed the plantations. In the middle of the eighteenth century Riau got gambir from Sumatra (used for the manufacture of cutch) for Chinese to plant, which made the island very prosperous, and from Riau its cultivation spread in the last century to Johore. Cloves flourished once under the British on the island of Penang, and in 1842 the nutmegs and mace exported from the Straits Settlements more than equalled the whole consumption of Great Britain, but in those days there was no scientific knowledge to combat pests. Pests and overproduction killed the coffee of Malaya. Millet will grow, and maize; if only the Malay and Chinese races would turn from rice to maize, which grows easily and without irrigation, Malaya's food problem might be solved locally. Sugar, patchouli, citronella and lemon-grass were all tried before para-rubber absorbed undivided attention. Kapok or the silk-cotton flourishes, but its cotton, which makes stuffing for life-belts and mattresses, is imported in quantity from Java. The fall in the price of rubber won a cursory interest for sisal, Mauritius and Manila hemps and rosella. Ground-nuts are grown as a local foodstuff. Fruit-trees of many kinds abound, though except for the indigenous durian and the banana, the fruit is not as fine as that produced by the volcanic soil of Java and by Dutch agricultural science. Oil-palms have been introduced on 31 British estates and suffer only from a fluctuating market.

Older probably than any of Malaya's industries, except fishing and perhaps the rice-planting in northern Malaya, is the mining of tin and of gold. Four times in history there has been an abnormal demand for tin: firstly in the age of bronze, of which it is a component, then by the Indian for his Hindu images, then by Europe for pewter-ware and now by the world for canning and motor-cars. The latest theory would discover Malaya's earliest miners of tin in the Yue and Cham of Indo-China, Mon-speaking people whose language has left many loan-words in Sakai dialects. To them are ascribed what the Malays term "Siamese" pits in Perak and in Pahang and workings at Kenaboi in Jelebu where bronze celts have been unearthed. Whoever these men of the Bronze Age were, the linguistic evidence suggests that they came by way of the Lebir, Pahang and Tembeling Rivers, and their arrival must have occurred a few centuries before Christ. Their successors were Indian miners as attested by Perak's Buddhist bronze images dating from the fifth to the ninth century A.D. Then Arabs came to buy the metal. Two Abbaside coins of the ninth century, unearthed in a jar at Sungai Bujang, corroborate Arab geographers who record visits of their countrymen to Kedah in that century in quest of tin. From the beginning of Malay rule in Malacca blocks of tin weighing about 2 lb. served as a clumsy currency. And Tomé Pires tells us how it was in tin that the chiefs of every western estuary from the Perak down to the Bernam paid annual tribute to the Sultans of Malacca. The Portuguese and Achinese in succession exacted tribute of tin from Perak. In 1649 the Dutch East India Company collected in Malacca the "extraordinary" quantity of 344 tons of tin, mostly from Perak. Nor is there mention of a larger output until free trade, established at Penang in 1786, gave such a fillip to mining in Perak that by 1839 Newbold estimated the output at 600 tons, still a pigmy prelude to the 26,000 tons of Malayan tin in 1889, the 50,000 tons (or 55·6 of the world's then output) in 1904, the 70,000 tons allocated to Malaya in 1937 under the International Producers' Restriction Scheme, and its potential modern output of 100,000 tons. Restriction was introduced to remedy overproduction, which had reduced the price of the metal from £284 a ton in 1926 to £144 in 1930, a figure below cost price. By Newbold's day there were Chinese mining everywhere, but especially in Larut and in Selangor, some on land leased by themselves, others for tribute on land owned by Malay chiefs. Even in 1912 80 per cent of the mining was in Chinese hands and in 1941 Chinese owned one-third of the mines. It was not till the end of the nineteenth century that some European capital was introduced for the installation of Western machinery. The Chinese form of mining was "open-cast"; that is, excavation by hand labour. Western methods include water monitors (like cannons) that wash down a hill face, and, latest device of all, bucket-dredges which, set on a pontoon, scrape up the swampy earth and drop it into sluices that extract the ore. There are only a few lode mines, the most famous at Sungai Lembing in Pahang. Malaya still produces more than one-third of the world's output and in 1955 the total capital invested was more than £13 million. The price of tin during this century has varied from £144 a ton in 1930 to £1,600 a ton during the Korean War. Practically all the ore has hitherto been smelted by two British companies at Singapore and Penang, an American attempt in 1902 to convey it to the United States as ballast and smelt it there having been thwarted by the imposition of a prohibitive export duty on the unsmelted ore.

Gold-mining also goes back to prehistoric times. The earliest miners would seem to have been the Mon-speaking immigrants of the Bronze Age, who opened gold mines in Pahang and, to judge from the absence of Indian remains, may have long continued mining in a country devoid of inhabitants other than aboriginal hill-men and a few hinduized Malays on the estuaries, whose trafficking in the gold made Pahang the most important region in the peninsula between the fall of Sri Vijaya and the rise of Malacca. From ruins of a tenth-century temple in Kedah have been unearthed a model bowl, a model lotus and a model lion, all in gold, articles which, though Indian in origin, may have been made of local metal, seeing that the quest for gold was one of the objects that led to Indian immigration. In the fifteenth century Pahang paid annual tribute of 5 lb. of its gold dust to Malacca. A Chinese Muslim, Fei Hsin, writing in 1436, tells how girls of rich Pahang families wore four or five golden circlets on their foreheads. From about 1550 Minangkabaus accustomed to gold-mining in Sumatra crossed the peninsula and started to mine for the metal along the Jelai in Pahang. Alluvial gold occurs in most of the Malay States, though not in sufficient quantity to attract even the Malays in these days of more profitable industries. There is one European gold mine, namely at Raub in Pahang. The mean annual value of gold won in Malaya between 1934 and 1938 was £234,311.

In the present century the Japanese opened iron mines in Johore and Trengganu, which in 1938 produced ore worth £858,319. It was the latest of Malaya's mining industries, but in 1956 the ore exported was valued at nearly £6 million.

So much for the pursuits of the landsman. But, as we have seen, from time immemorial there have been Malays who turned to the sea for their livelihood and devoted nearly all their time to fishing, which of all Malay industries is the most specialized.

Hook-and-line fishing is highly developed, with or without rod, by night lines and with long lines of hooks. From the Johore causeway Malays on a breezy day will angle for the belone (of the garfish tribe) with a kite from which dangles a line with a baited noose. But even line fishing, though not a method of modern industry, was new to the aborigines of Singapore when Raffles acquired a site there, and the wooden fish spear or *sĕligi* which those sea-gipsies used has survived in the name of a street in the great modern city.

Upcountry Malays set in the rivers traps of the same type as our eel-traps, some with inner compartments to prevent egress, others of thorny twigs with barbed points that deter the catch from returning upstream to liberty. There are square and conical traps, where the tug of a fish dislodges a catch and drops a door. Bait may be used or weirs, dams and converging lines of screens to induce or force the fish to enter the trap.

The three main types of large sea fish-traps or stakes are a development of the riverine traps. In the first the fish are headed by converging rows of stakes into a large enclosure where there is a submerged screen; this bamboo screen is raised by a windlass and the fish are caught. In the second type fish are headed into successive compartments of diminishing size, to be picked out of the inmost by landing-baskets or to be left there high and dry by the receding tide. In the third and simplest type a tidal creek is enclosed temporarily by a fence of rattan so that the fall of the tide leaves the fish high and dry. All these are commercial methods.

The fishing-nets used in Malayan waters may be divided into floating or drift-nets, drag-nets, casting-nets, fixed purse-nets, ground or lift-nets. The casting-net that resembles the net of the gladiator bears a Sanskrit name. A bag-net (too small for commercial purposes) was bequeathed to the Malacca fisherman by the Portuguese. The ordinary seine-net is sometimes called the Chinese net. The debt the Malay fisherman may owe to India (or India to the Malay fishermen) has not been explored. Even in Malayan waters there are local differences in traps, nets and methods. On the east coast a medicine-man enters the water and swims about, diving and listening to locate a shoal and determine the kind of fish in the neighbourhood, so that his comrades may not heave their great net into the sea to no purpose. The medicine-man will control perhaps twenty nets, each boat having a crew that may be as low as five or as high as nine. In his exhaustive study of the economy of the Kelantan fisherman (a pioneer volume of the greatest value to the administrator) Professor Raymond Firth explains how "in each lift-net crew there is a fairly stable nucleus, consisting mainly of the boat captains, their kinsfolk and close friends or neighbours. When the number of nets is small, there is a reserve of labour, in which the semi-independent fishermen are one element. But when the number of nets increases, this reserve disappears and part-time agriculturists and independent fishermen are enlisted where possible." Even in their most highly specialized industry the Malays are some of them amateurs.

The European expert dismisses both the Malay and Chinese fisherman of Malaya as practising methods that obtained at the time of the Apostles, and therefore fit to be studied only by the ethnographer. But in spite of antiquated methods the size of the industry is by no means insignificant, though it is always liable to suffer from the natural preference of the Malay for any more profitable means of livelihood. From Trengganu, with its long coast-line, a state where about ten per cent of the small population are fishermen, the average value of fish exported annually before the war was more than £100,000, a figure that excluded the value of fish eaten by the local population. The total annual catch by Malaya's 50,000 fishermen was then estimated at wholesale prices as worth nearly £1 million. For the net earnings of Malaya's 10,000-odd Chinese fishermen no statistics are available, but the individual Malay fisherman earned before the war £1 a month on the east coast and £1 6s. on the west: a miserable pittance compared with the £16 or £20 a month got by a Malay with five acres of rubber, although a not inadequate return on the fisherman's capital expenditure of £5. Moreover, even the professional fisherman does not depend wholly on fishing, both food and cash accruing to him from the coconuts, arecanuts and vegetables of his garden. Besides, before the war a Kelantan or Trengganu fisherman with a family of three required to spend only 11d. a month on rice and clothes and sundries. He led a free independent healthy life that the clerk or shop assistant of Europe may well envy, although the conditions of Malay fisheries used to be neglected by the government and needed certain radical improvements. In the first place, as only in Kelantan and Trengganu has the foreigner been kept from exploiting the local fisherman and monopolizing fish-dealing, the Malay fisherman must be brought to realize the value of co-operative societies so that so large a percentage of his earnings may no longer pass to the Chinese fish-curer who puts up the capital for so many fish-stakes and so many boats. In the second place there was needed some mechanization of the industry, with the introduction of powered craft such as Japanese fishermen used in Malayan waters to reach remoter fishing-grounds. Then again, although land transport enabled the Kuantan fisherman to transport (or let a Chinese transport) his catch to the Kuala Lumpor market, yet ice-boats were needed as tenders on the fleets so that the fisherman might not be forced to sell nearly all his catch to the curer but get the higher price for the fresh fish.

By 1956 the Fisheries Department had done very much to

improve the industry. One-third of the fishing-boats in the Federation were motorized. New roads on the East Coast helped distribution. In Kelantan a co-operative marketing scheme was proving popular. The retail value of the 22,216 tons of fish caught off the Federated States in 1956 was just over £15½ million. The amount of local fish caught off Singapore and auctioned there was 4260·3 tons in 1954 and 4358·5 tons in 1955.

CHAPTER XIII

LABOUR: HEALTH: EDUCATION:

i. Labour

APART from justice, the merits of any modern government are judged mainly by its care for labour, health and education.

Care for labour did not exist in Malaya before the British period any more than it existed in France before the Revolution of 1793. To make the position worse, the Malays had brought with them on their descent from Yunnan the institution of slavery, long before they were influenced by Hindu ideas. Ownership of slaves and bondsmen was the mark of wealth, rank and power. Slaves included prisoners of war, pagan aborigines snared "like chimpanzees", murderers who, unable to pay the blood-price, bartered liberty for sanctuary with the ruler, the children of female slaves other than those acknowledged by their owners, Batak and Balinese bought in mediaeval Malacca and in early Penang, Abyssinian and negro slaves smuggled back from Mecca in the guise of servants. Most iniquitous, perhaps, was the case of the debt-bondsman, whose work in his creditor's house, field or mine was never set against the sum he owed and who often had to feed and clothe himself. Sometimes the desire of a chief or his wife to possess the services of a particular person led to his or her enslavement on the score of a debt entirely fictitious. With brutal logic Malay law laid it down that the hiring of a slave was like the borrowing of a stick and the borrower had the same responsibility for the safety of slave or debt-bondsman as he had for the safety of a buffalo. Only in Negri Sembilan was debt slavery rare, the tribe defraying a tribesman's debts rather than lose his services.

There was yet another way of solving the problem of domestic service at the expense of the liberty of the subject. On the occasion of a royal marriage or birth a Sultan would have young women carried off to be maids or nurses. If they were unmarried they became courtesans about the palace; if they were married their husbands, too, became royal slaves.

As in many Eastern countries, the Malay freeman also had to render feudal service as a tenant of the ruler. He was recruited to build a palace, to make roads and drains, to tend elephants, pole boats and cultivate the royal domain and to fight as a soldier. The hardships endured is the burden of many pages in *Abdullah's Voyage to the East Coast in 1851*. The corvée for all this forced labour was organized by village headmen, who executed orders without forgetting their own interests as they fined the recalcitrant and pocketed bribes to grant exemptions.

Slaves figured among the imports into Malacca from its foundation down to the last century. After its capture by d'Albuquerque in 1511 the Portuguese kept many slaves. When the Dutch conquered the port in 1641 one Portuguese, Pedro Dabreu, surrendered along with 200 slaves, of whom 60 were kept for building, the rest incapable of work being left outside the city to erect their own houses. In the confusion of the siege the Minangkabaus of Naning and Rembau seized many slaves, some of them Christians. The Dutch tried hard to recover the Christians and on one occasion got back six of them along with one silver candlestick, two silver spoons, one Spanish cassock, one undergarment and one red doublet. In addition to its own 185 slaves the Dutch Company in 1678 was hiring private slaves at as much as eight to ten stivers a day, as their owners took advantage of a labour shortage. Slaves accompanied Dutch punitive expeditions into the interior.

In 1786 the Dutch port officer at Malacca could not tell the number of his own slaves, but it was over 60. In 1795 when the British took over Malacca, the Governor's wife entertained the officers, playing on her harp with some of her slaves accompanying her on violins. In his will dated 1795 Francis Light, the founder of Penang, left sums to two female slaves he had freed, bequeathed all his Batak slaves to Martina Rozells and all his *kafir* slaves, too, if she wanted them, and released from further bondage seven Chinese slaves and their children. And though Singapore was founded after an Act of Parliament had declared the keeping of slaves a felony, its first Resident had winked at the trade. It was Stamford Raffles who took the lead in abolishing slavery. All slaves imported after the establishment of Singapore were given by him the right to claim their freedom. Needless to add, in the last quarter of the nineteenth century, as each Malay State came under British protection, slavery was extirpated, without protest.

Even free labour may suffer from exploitation. But what a change came with the present century! In some respects the Malayan attitude towards labour anticipated the policy laid down by Geneva. This enlightened attitude was due perhaps less to altruism than to the country's dependence on foreign labour for the great tin and rubber industries, which in 1937 employed 300,000 Indians, 200,000 Chinese, 30,000 Malays and 15,000 Javanese. A Labour Code, often amended, forbade the truck system (or payment in kind), prescribed a maternity allowance and leave for women, required employers to pay hospital fees for coolies and their families, to provide crêches for infants and schools for children (who might not be employed under ten), and to pay a minimum wage that would cover a trip to India every three years. 1910 saw the abolition of indentured labour, 1922 the abolition of penal sanctions for labour offences and 1937 such a voluntary flow of labour that 88·8 per cent of the Indian males who came to Malaya that year had not been recruited.

The Chinese labourer neither needed nor welcomed so much interference by the government. No minimum wage was prescribed, for he always got higher pay than the Indian. He preferred the chances of piece-work to the certainty of a fixed wage. But as he was not so qualified to protect his interests as he imagined, the government was quick to legislate against abuses.

Guilds were traditional for Indian and Chinese labourers, but in 1940 the government legislated for the organization of trade unions and after the war helped labourers to form them.

Probably the one measure open to criticism in the actions of the Malayan governments was the repatriation of unemployed labourers during the 1929 slump. It cost millions of dollars, but it may be argued that in the time of booms money should be set aside for the rainy day. It is, however, a difficult problem, as the

LABOUR; HEALTH; EDUCATION 127

majority of coolies would themselves desire to take advantage of a slump for visiting their homelands.

In 1940 some 67,000 Indian labourers owned £285,000 in co-operative societies. For in 1921 the governments started a department to encourage and assist such societies in order to help agriculturists to get better prices for their crops and to rescue labourers and clerks from a burden of debt. At the end of 1956 the Federation had more than 2,000 societies with over 240,000 members and a working capital of £8,385,427.

ii. HEALTH

Alike for labourers and for all classes and races, British medicine has been an incalculable boon, modern science taking the place of mediaeval guesswork. Disease, according to the Malay notion, was due to the attack of some spirit or to the machinations of an enemy over some part of the patient's body; for example, the clippings of hair or nails. Bathing, one might offend some nature spirit. Hunting, one might be struck down by the malignant aura of slain deer or pig or bird, to be counteracted by smearing one's body with clay and so putting oneself under the protection of the earth-spirit as a Greek actor put himself under the protection of the god of wine by daubing his face with wine lees. A woman might be harmed by the bottle-imp familiar of a rival. Especially baneful to women were the banshees of those who died in childbirth. Younger than banshees, bottle-imps and nature-spirits are the djinns of Islam, the Malay's latest faith. Again, "Just as Plato ascribed disease to disturbances of the balance of power between the four properties of earth, air, fire and water, out of which the body is compacted, so the Malay ascribed all diseases to the four classes of genies presiding over those properties. The genies of the air cause wind-borne complaints: dropsy, blindness, hemiplegia and insanity. The genies of the black earth cause vertigo, with sudden blackness of vision. The genies of fire cause hot fevers and yellow jaundice. The white genies of the sea cause chill, catarrhs and agues." The Malay brought his most primitive ideas of disease from central Asia and borrowed later notions from contact first with Hindus and then with Indian Muslims who had got second-hand from Arabia some knowledge of Greek medical theory.

The Malay knew nothing of surgery, though he could treat simple fractures. In cases of serious illness diagnosis is made by a village shaman's *séance*, where Siva is still often invoked to discover what spirit is causing the sickness and what offering that spirit demands. For milder complaints the ordinary village medicine-man employs a simple clinical method based on experience, but sometimes rendered impressive by pretence of divination. His curative medicine consists of contagious or homoeopathic magic, of placatory offerings, of spoken and written charms, of herbal remedies and of diet to restore the balance between the four natural properties heat and cold, dryness and moisture. A patient may be rubbed with bezoar-stone to acquire the vitality of its strong soul-substance. The placatory offering may be waved over a sufferer or hung up in a tray or set adrift in a spirit-boat. The charm or incantation appears to have spread through Asia from some early centre like Babylon, but in Malaya was further popularized by borrowings from Hindu and Muslim India. The Malay pharmacopoeia of herbs must have taken thousands of years of empirical research to collect. But just as the great bulk of Malay literature consists of translations, so the greater part of the Malay's prescriptions appear to have been borrowed. As once in British therapeutics, the pomegranate is used for tape-worm, but the pomegranate came from India. It is possible that many of the plants that have provided drugs for the Malay were brought from India. The word for long pepper, which has febrifuge, stomachic and anti-spasmodic properties, is Sanskrit. The word for coriander is Tamil, and as in India it is taken for coughs. The sandalwood-tree is indigenous in the East Indies, but it bears a Sanskrit name; it was perhaps from Indians that Malays learnt of its value as an astringent and for stomachic pains. Cummin, employed as a diuretic by Indians and Malays, came from Persia. Senna was imported from Arabia to India less than two centuries ago and from India to Malaya. It is clear that, provided he is given time to assimilate new ideas, the Malay is not averse to change in medical practice. I myself have seen the entire population of one of the beautiful but malarial islands off Pahang swarm round a government launch to ask for quinine, and when told that the stock was exhausted they finished a huge bottle of black draught as better than nothing. It is only surgery that the Malay dreads and his religion condemns.

The medicine of India and China was as mediaeval as the Malay. Though China discovered ephedrine to be a specific for asthma, its druggists, to the delight of pre-historians, stock mastodons' teeth. So in such a field as Malaya European medicine had a chance to work wonders. Not that it sprang up fully equipped like Minerva from the head of Jove. Penang had existed for close on twenty years before it got medical officers, and it was proposed that Indian convicts should be employed as nurses. Even where there were British doctors, the death-rate was, for many years, terrific. Stamford Raffles, for example, lost a wife and all but one of his children. The Malays had long guessed that malaria was due to the mosquito, but we find a Singapore physician writing on coral-reefs as its cause, and it was not till the last quarter of the nineteenth century that quinine was commonly prescribed as a specific. Sometimes the discovery of a remedy was due to a lucky chance, as 606 proved to be a cure for yaws. Progress might have been quicker but for a lack of international co-operation. Take beri-beri, which the Chinese mention as long ago as the seventh century. In 1896 a Dutch doctor in Java had noticed that chickens fed on polished rice were liable to this disease, and published a paper. But when more than ten years later British doctors made the discovery in Malaya that beri-beri was caused by a deficiency in diet they were unaware of the work of Dr. Eykman and there was a dispute between two of them as to which was the pioneer discoverer!

Greater even than their curative medicine have been the measures taken by British doctors to prevent tropical diseases, especially malaria. In 1898 Sir Ronald Ross, studying the mosquito under the microscope, discovered the importance of knowing the insect's life history in order to stamp out a fever that causes more deaths and more illness than all other diseases put together. In 1901 (Sir) Malcolm Watson started to show the value of draining swamps where mosquitoes breed. But the way of research is full of pitfalls. And it was more than a decade before it was proved to be a mistake to clear ravines of bushes that kept the anopheles close to the clear stream where they breed. But anti-malarial work in Malaya earned a world-wide reputation. Before the Japanese occupation the disease had been banished from all the larger towns and from most estates (whose owners recognized the value of healthy labour), though it could not be eradicated except at quite prohibitive cost from terraced rice-fields in isolated valleys. It is possible that time will bring new methods of exterminating the anopheles.

With the growth of towns tuberculosis is a most serious menace to their inhabitants.

iii. EDUCATION

To the modern mind education does not exist without school buildings, though to mediaeval man it was the teacher who mattered more than the desk. At least as early as A.D. 671 there were Indian teachers in the Malay world, when a Chinese Buddhist, I-tsing, spent six months at the capital of Sri Vijaya studying Sanskrit, as Chinese were wont to do for a year or so before sailing on to India. Then at the end of the thirteenth century Islam, spreading from Pasai (in modern Acheh), brought a new alphabet and literature. Two centuries later the author of the *Malay Annals*, writing in Malacca, is familiar with Sanskrit, Persian and Tamil, with Javanese literature and Kuranic texts. He professes also a smattering of Chinese, Siamese and Portuguese. He knows the Ramayana and apparently the Mahabharata. He has read Malay translations of the Muslim romances of Alexander the Great, Muhammad Hanafiah and Amir Hamzah. He is acquainted with the doctrines of Sufi mystics. Clearly there were means of acquiring knowledge in old Malacca. The *Annals* tell us how the Sultans sat at the feet of missionaries from India, who sometimes pretended to have come from Mecca, and how irritated those missionaries got with pupils who were slow at pronouncing Arabic, and how angry with courtiers who laughed at their own efforts to speak Malay.

LABOUR; HEALTH; EDUCATION 131

For centuries there were several definite types of Malay education. There was the training of the ordinary peasant, boys and girls learning from their parents fishing, trapping, agriculture, weaving and cookery. In proverbs and folk-lore the girls were perhaps better instructed than the boys. Under the influence of the hinduized courts a few youths learned to work in brass, silver and gold, and others to make weapons, though they were all agriculturists in season and not complete specialists. Then there was the training of the young raja who learnt to read the Kuran and to fence and was instructed in astrology and magical formulae to gain invulnerability and achieve success in love and war. There was also the training of the shaman's pupil in the cultivation of visual hallucinations and the special education of the village medicine-man who studied charms and the traditional properties of herbs. Finally there was the education of the Malay scholar, which till modern times meant the education of the Muslim theologian. Any boy anxious to learn the Kuran and understand the general drift of the text went to live with a teacher, whom he helped in house and field. Even today the few who feel the call of religion strongly do not study English, but, having learnt all they can from some local teacher, go to Mecca or to al-Azhar University at Cairo, there to acquire Arabic and Muslim theology, which to their minds includes all knowledge. Every Malay boy and girl still has to learn to chant the Kuran from cover to cover in a language he does not understand, and this gruelling task hardly furthers his advancement in the English schools.

The education of foreign settlers in Malaya belonged before the nineteenth century to the cultural history of India and China. And in Malacca the Catholics kept open school for their small Eurasian flock.

Then, in 1823, twenty-three years before any annual grant towards education was made in England, Sir Stamford Raffles laid in Singapore the foundation stone of an Institution that still bears his name. On behalf of the East India Company he endowed it with a grant of $300 a month and a large area of valuable land, endowments dissipated as the years went by. The Institution was to have literary and moral departments for Chinese, Malays and Siamese and a scientific department for the common advantage of the several colleges that might be constituted. Raffles clearly knew nothing of educational organization and expected his students to run before they could walk. So it is not surprising that in 1827 the Bengal government decided to apply the grant solely to the establishment of elementary schools. Ten years later an abortive attempt was made to use the Institution for its founder's purpose, but it is hardly a matter for wonder that the Chinese pupils fell away and the Malays displayed apathy at the study of the history of Greece and Rome, chronology, natural philosophy, trigonometry and the use of globes. From 1844 till 1871 the building housed a school for girls. Then in 1870 a Cambridge graduate was engaged as Principal and the modern history of the Institution began. The Trustees tried to turn it into a high school with science classes to be fed from the city's six elementary schools. But the original endowments had been wasted, and in 1903 the government took it over and made it a secondary school. Its history is interesting as an epitome of the stumbles and falls and advancement of education in Malaya. The differentiation between education in English and education in vernaculars, and between an elementary and a secondary school, the outlining of a curriculum fitted to local needs, the education of girls, the teaching of science, the provision of a college for the sons of Malay chiefs, the difficulty of getting suitable masters, the problem of aided and of government schools are all of them matters that cropped up in later days.

In 1872 an Inspector of Schools was appointed, whose title was changed in 1901 into Director of Public Instruction for the Straits Settlements, and later to Director of Education. That Inspector inaugurated an educational system whose development may be traced in (*a*) the gradual recruitment of an adequate and efficient staff for an Education Department, (*b*) increasing financial provision for government and missionary schools, mainly as a result of the representations of that department, and (*c*) in the development of curricula on lines of higher proficiency and greater specialization.

Today primary education is given throughout Malaya in English, Malay, Chinese and Indian schools. The Malay vernacular schools, which are free and maintained by govern-

LABOUR; HEALTH; EDUCATION 133

ment, prepare the brighter boys for entry to English schools and give those who prefer village life instruction in the three Rs, geography, Malay history, tropical hygiene, gardening, poultry-keeping and general handiwork. Malay girls study the same subjects with suitable modifications. In contrast to the Malay schools, Chinese vernacular schools have been largely endowed or self-supporting and self-governing, though schools accommodating about half the pupils enrolled received government grants before the Japanese war. Down to the '20s they taught the Old Style Chinese learning, till influenced by the Revolution they adopted the New Mandarin and text-books too nationalist in tone to make for the children's adaptation to their Malayan environment. Interference by the Education Department was, however, resented except when Communist students occasionally locked up the staff of a school and assistance was invoked to release the teachers. At nearly all these Chinese vernacular schools some English was taught, usually badly, to meet the popular demand. Indian schools are mostly situated on rubber estates and the teaching is generally in Tamil. Their main difficulty is to recruit competent teachers. But if the schools are efficient they also receive grants-in-aid.

The English schools of Malaya were those in which English was the sole medium of instruction, though they admitted pupils of every race, the majority of them Chinese. Many of the schools are conducted by missionary bodies who receive grants-in-aid to cover any deficit. The aim of the secondary schools is to produce youths and girls who shall pass the Cambridge School Certificate examination. Three-quarters of the staffs of the English schools are Chinese, Eurasians, Malays and others of local birth.

In independent Malaya both Malay and English are compulsory in all primary and secondary schools, the former to give instruction in other languages when needed. Admission to the national-type secondary schools is by competitive examination.

In September 1956 the Federation had 4878 schools with 972,665 pupils. Of that total 398,412 pupils were studying Malay as their principal language, 320,168 Chinese, 205,563 English and 58,522 Indian languages. In 1955 Singapore had

E

662 schools with 212,237 pupils. Instruction in primary schools is given in English, Malay, Chinese or Tamil, and some agitation for secondary education to be given through the medium of Malay was frustrated by the lack of competent teachers.

In addition to these schools for general education, there are Trade (or Artisan) Schools for the training of mechanics, blacksmiths, plumbers, electricians, carpenters and tailors. At Kuala Lumpor there is a Technical College providing courses in surveying and the various forms of engineering required for posts in the technical departments. An Agricultural College at Serdang provides a three years' course in English and a one year's course in Malay for the study of tropical agriculture.

After the Japanese war a University of Malaya was started by combining King Edward VII College of Medicine and Raffles College, both at Singapore, and it still exists as the University of Singapore. Students passing out of the Medical Faculty are qualified to practise anywhere in the British Empire. Students passing out from the other faculties enter the local civil services, especially the educational department. The University of Malaya was supported by annual grants from the Federation and Singapore, the former contributing 60 per cent of the total. The Cambridge Higher Certificate is the basis for admission. In 1956 there were 1574 students, 930 of them Chinese, 360 Indians and Ceylonese, 213 Malays and 36 Eurasians. The engineering and agricultural and some other faculties were transferred to Kuala Lumpur where a division of the University was opened.

In 1956 the Federation had over 1000 private and 602 aided students abroad—Singapore had 157 aided and many private students in the United Kingdom, Australia and the United States.

After the Malay States with Penang and Malacca became an independent federation and Singapore had separate self-government, a second University of Malaya was founded at Kuala Lumpur.

CHAPTER XIV

JAPAN'S HOUR OF TRIUMPH

IN AUGUST 1941 Japanese troops poured into the south of Indo-China and reached the new frontier of Siam. On 8 December Japan declared war on Great Britain and the United States of America. On the same day her forces raided Manila, sank the bulk of the American fleet at Pearl Harbour, bombed Singapore at 4 a.m., marched into Bangkok, captured Malaya's northernmost aerodrome in Kelantan and landed on the beaches near Kota Baharu. The next day, 9 December, saw Admiral Phillips' forlorn attempt to halt the sea-borne invasion by taking the *Prince of Wales* and the *Repulse* up the Gulf of Siam under monsoon clouds but without air-cover. On 10 December, the lowering grey clouds broke long enough to let the Japanese sink both ships and shatter British sea-power in the Pacific as American sea-power had been shattered two days earlier at Pearl Harbour.

By 13 December the main Japanese army had smashed the British prepared position at Jitra in the north of Kedah and started its descent of 550 miles down the main arterial road to Singapore at the average rate of ten miles a day. Japan employed at least 150,000 men on the campaign, had about 300 bombers and 400 fighters (against our 141 obsolete planes), and some 300 tanks, a weapon with which for reasons unexplained our troops were not equipped. The Japanese tactics were as monotonous as the tactics their spies had employed at tennis tournaments in peace-time Singapore, and even more effective. Confronted with an obstacle on their march, they disappeared into the jungle on both sides of the road, came out south of it and encircled it, or they got below it as at Kuala Kangsar by following some by-road, or as at Kampar by sending forces round by sea to the rear of our defence. From Kampar the British and Indian forces had to retire, having been outflanked by the Japanese, who landed south of them on the Bernam River and were about to encircle them from Teluk

Anson. The Division was to halt at Slim River and was expected to make a stand there. But, worn out by three weeks' continuous fighting, our battalions were cut to pieces.

On 9 January, 1942, General Wavell visited the front. He can have needed no more than a glance at the map and Selangor's network of roads to order retreat past Kuala Lumpor, 125 miles south down to the Muar River, the last obstacle except a strip of sea between the enemy and Singapore. All the Malay States were now to be abandoned except the southernmost, Johore. Eye-witnesses have described the bizarre procession of lorries, cars, trollies, ambulances, ordnance vans, tractors, eleven steam-rollers and two fire-engines that crept along the granite roads of Selangor and Negri Sembilan past groups of villagers who stood stunned and bewildered. It was as if the Japanese themselves could not believe their good fortune. The fugitives, many asleep from fatigue, moved unmolested. No bombs were dropped. Not a bridge was blown up.

Nothing could halt the invader now, but it was the turn of the Australian Imperial Forces to strike a blow. There was a flicker of phantom hope that somehow the Australians, who had not so far gone into action, would accomplish the impossible and retrieve the hour. They ambushed the Japanese at a bridge which they blew up near Gemas and they destroyed some thousand of them for the loss of less than eighty Australians killed and wounded. Except for this one engagement the defence never had air-cover, though it had always been the intention to defend Malaya from the air. But of what use was a successful ambush when Britain's forces were too small to wrest the initiative by counter-attack?

The Japanese advance continued without halt, inexorable. The main body of the enemy arrived at Muar and after a battle of six days crossed the river that was its last obstacle on the mainland, pushing back an Indian brigade and compelling the Australians at Gemas to retreat hurriedly across the one bridge on the Segamat River to avoid encirclement. Bodies of our men were cut off from time to time. On the coast the Japanese had landed at Batu Pahat. The main Japanese army now pressed confidently forward by road and railway.

On 25 January, 1942, it was decided to withdraw all the

British forces to Singapore island on the night of 30–31 January. The enemy did not interfere with this operation, desiring probably to let Singapore be crowded to confusion and to have all his prisoners together in one bag.

The last regiment to quit the mainland was the Argyll and Sutherland Highlanders, a remnant of 200 out of 850 men, who crossed the causeway at night with the pipes playing "Blue Bonnets over the Border". It was one of those gestures which bring tears of pride to the eyes and create a nation, but which generally should bring tears of shame for lives thrown away.

An incredible war of outposts General Gordon Bennett called the Malayan campaign, but it was almost over now, though many failed to recognize the end was so near. When the troops reached Singapore, the naval base that had cost £30,000,000 had been destroyed by British engineers and at sea the *Empress of Asia* had been set on fire by enemy bombers. The Japanese began to shell and bomb what was more like an open cattle-pen than an impregnable fortress. On 8 February they started to bomb intensively the north-west corner of the island, the one place where their troops could land under cover. At 10 p.m. they disembarked 23,000 men there in a mangrove swamp. By 11 February Japanese tanks had reached Bukit Timah in the middle of the island. Two days later military opinion was unanimous that further resistance was useless, but General Wavell ordered a fight to the end. Although 36,000 fresh untrained troops had just been landed (from an optimism unjustifiable) they were inexperienced and there was no labour to unload their equipment under the threat of Japanese bombs. The troops that had fought from Siam down the length of the peninsula were an exhausted remnant. Munition and food were giving out and, above all, the water-supply was cut. On 15 February, 1942, a white flag was hoisted on Government House and the British surrendered unconditionally.

Of the conduct of the Malayan campaign there has been much criticism, some professional, much irrelevant. One soldier wonders if the British did not miss victory at the first encounter near Kota Baharu by failing to hold fast. This clearly is to underestimate the strength and doggedness of the Japanese.

Perhaps the British position at Jitra was tactically unsound, constituted as it was mainly of open rice-fields with flanks strung out so far that the centre was weak, but not far enough to prevent encirclement. Perhaps the position at Gurun was better. But what was known of jungle warfare then? Long-range artillery becomes useless where the field of vision is restricted by trees, and having no tanks British tacticians sought positions where artillery was of value. Besides, how could the British forces face the jungle, when even a tough realist like General Gordon Bennett could write how "enormous snakes hang on the undergrowth or slither along the ground. Cobras, pythons, hamadryads and the dangerously poisonous krait show themselves. Hornets and scorpions abound. Mangy, smelly tigers, dangerous sladangs who will charge blindly into any humans in their vicinity—all these give horror to the jungle." The Malay regiments and the local volunteers, all of whom would have been delighted to see a sladang and tackled any cobra with a split bamboo, were kept for the greater part of the campaign as separate units, instead of being attached as guides to the British and Indian regiments. There was no one the British soldier or the Indian could trust to tell him how to distinguish between a Malay and a Japanese in a Malay *sarong*. The tactic of trying to throw a thin line of defence athwart the main road failed all down the peninsula. It was like a man barring his front door against burglars and leaving open the ground-floor windows. One man surprised by burglars may have no choice; two or three inmates could close the windows and open the door, ambushing the burglars in the passage and banging them over the head if they dared to enter. That was what the Australians did at Gemas, but then, as always, our forces were too weak to exchange defence for attack. Against 600,000 troops in Burma there were 125,000 in Malaya, too few ever to start an offensive, even if the British had then known the way. Not only did the troops lack an air arm and protection from sea-landings in their rear; they had a high percentage of unseasoned men and untrained officers. As early as 16 December, the Australian G.O.C., General Bennett, wrote: "I spent much time studying the serious position of Malaya and realized that nothing could save the country

JAPAN'S HOUR OF TRIUMPH 139

unless reinforcements of experienced troops of good fighting quality should arrive at an early date."

The loss of Malaya is acknowledged to have been a purely military disaster. But naturally the soldier and the civilian look back for the primary cause of defeat. "It is the duty of the statesman to assemble a superior force at the decisive moment at the right spot." By that criterion it was the fault of the British statesman that Malaya was overwhelmed by a cataclysm whose repercussions in the Far East were incalculable. But the War Cabinet of the day had an excuse. "I submit," said Mr. Churchill, "that the main strategic and political decision to aid Russia, to deliver an offensive in Libya and to accept a consequential state of weakness in the then peaceful theatre of the Far East, was sound." The House of Commons concurred. Some argued that the Malays, and especially the Chinese, should have been armed and trained to defend the peninsula. But by the time world opinion would have condoned such a course the hour for it had passed and equipment was wanting. Besides, though the Malay Regiment fought most gallantly, the relations between Chinese communist guerillas and the Malays before and after the British recovery of Malaya are evidence of the grave risk of arming a population of mixed races, many not British subjects. Others argued that years ago the Japanese should have been forbidden access to Malaya's coastal waters and jungle paths, not stopping to reflect that such a course would have been tantamount to inviting war. Journalists unnerved by the unimaginable disaster babbled of an inefficient civil service, dancing parties at the hotels and whisky-swilling planters. As conservators of precedent no civil service can function normally when precedents are flouted by armed force. There was a ball in the evening before Waterloo. And General Gordon Bennett, after extolling the civil servants and unofficials of Malaya, remarks that during a year there he saw no British man or woman under the influence of liquor and found less drunkenness than in England and Australia. What all races did for civil defence has been recorded.

CHAPTER XV

THE MALAYAN UNION AND SINGAPORE

BEFORE the Japanese invasion the Malays were probably the only people in Asia who as a race not only respected but felt affection for the British. The Strait-born Chinese entertained the same feeling, but they represent a community, not a race. Both the Malays and the Straits-born Chinese were wild with joy at our return and welcomed our troops with single-hearted gratitude. It might therefore have been expected that after failure to secure for the peoples of Malaya the protection that treaties had guaranteed the British would have healed their wounds and assuaged their hunger and even listened to their views before any thought of altering their treaties and giving officials new English designations irrelevant to good government and confusing for the local inhabitant. But instead of showing consideration for an unnerved people, Whitehall dashed into the recovered Malaya as Mr. Birch dashed into Perak in 1874, as if it were an Augean stable instead of a country that for half a century had been a model for the smooth administration of mixed races. The attempt to cleanse it was made in haste and with a measure of ignorant prejudice. For Whitehall felt quite groundlessly, with the example of Belgium, Holland, Denmark and Norway before it, that a strong centralized government might have done more than a patchwork federation to halt the Japanese conquest. There was also a mistaken notion that the Malays, disappointed at Britain's failure to protect them, had helped the invader. The new deal aimed therefore at bureaucratic efficiency, ignoring Malay sentiment altogether and tending to favour the Chinese who still except for the Communists respected as a mirror for administrators the ancient sage Shun, who "did nothing but governed well". So incubated in extreme secrecy (a tactic prompted by the war) Whitehall proceeded to sponsor a new policy for Malaya that compared

THE MALAYAN UNION AND SINGAPORE 141

with its last pre-war policy was another complete *volte-face*. For in 1933 the Colonial Office had published and accepted the following opinion of its then permanent head:

> "From a purely economic point of view it would no doubt be advisable in a country the size of Malaya to have one Central Government administering the whole territory. There is, however, the political aspect of the problem....
>
> "Moreover it seems clear that the maintenance of the position, authority and prestige of the Malay Rulers must always be a cardinal point in British policy; and the encouragement of indirect rule will probably prove the greatest safeguard against the political submersion of the Malays which would result from the development of popular government on western lines. For, in such a government the Malays would be hopelessly outnumbered by the other races owing to the great influx of immigrants that has taken place into Malaya during the last few years.
>
> "Politically everything seems to point to the desirability of the Rulers and their respective Governments being allowed to have control of their own domestic affairs without interference except in those cases where a unified policy is clearly necessary."

The new deal scorned this conclusion, lumping the protected Malay States along with the Settlements of Penang and Malacca into a Union under His Majesty's jurisdiction, with Singapore as the one relic of the Crown Colony of the Straits Settlements. In the new Union the states were no longer described as protectorates but as a protectorate. Rulers who had always presided at State Councils were no longer to be members, and the chair was to be taken by a British Resident Commissioner. Even the prerogative of mercy was no longer to be exercised by the Rulers. *Crown* grants were to be issued for unoccupied lands not by a High Commissioner but by a Governor as in a colony, and the laws were no longer, as heretofore, to be signed and ratified by the Sultans, but by that Governor whose very title symbolized the annexation of the protected states, or, let us say, their descent to a colonial status unprecedented for such highly organized and civilized countries. Jurisdiction, of course, means full powers of government from Whitehall. This in fact existed under the decent formula of the old treaties. But the new agreements, which the Sultans, taken by surprise and without time or leave to consult their people, were induced to sign, gave a blank cheque for the future disposal of the Malays, compelling them to accept "such future constitutional arrangements for Malaya as may be approved by His Majesty". One of these arrangements was that any Malay chief appointed a member of a State Council should swear allegiance not to his own Sultan but to the King of England. Humiliation could hardly go farther.

In clauses as vague as those that adumbrated a Crown-*cum*-protectorate Union, the new proposals talked of a Malayan franchise. Birth in Malaya or a period of residence there was to qualify Briton, Chinese and Indian to become citizens with "all the rights that term implies". What it does imply is not beyond legal and political cavil but it is hardly surprising that one of the Malay Rulers at once challenged a Whitehall statement that "Great Britain having learnt the richness of an infusion of new blood and talent", and having derived strength from it, was aiming at the same consummation in Malaya. "I would point out," wrote His Highness, "that Great Britain has never at any time accepted as citizens aliens equal in number to her indigenous population, and that such immigrations as have occurred have been of people closely related in blood and of the same religion, which is not the case with Chinese, Indians and the indigenous people of Malaya." The inadequacy of the official definition of this citizenship was pilloried in the House of Commons, but criticism left the Government unmoved (1947), although since a Chinese cannot change his nationality some of these citizens might one day be enemy nationals, and no paper stipulations could overcome the prospect that within a few years Chinese nationals might be outvoting and dominating all the other races in Malaya and turning a peninsula that is the key to the Pacific into a province of China. With their customary acceptance of the inevitable Malays agreed to this citizenship for foreigners who make Malaya their permanent home. But naturally they were nervous lest the consequent Chinese administrative service (1952) might prelude a change that would make Malays liable to be tried in their own country by a Chinese or Indian judge. Chinese and Indians had long had seats on the State and Federal Councils, and in the old Federated States they flooded the ranks of the subordinate civil service. But as early as 1904 the Rulers' objection to foreigners other than British in the higher posts of the civil service had been upheld by Whitehall. In the Colony of the Straits Settlements superior posts were thrown open some years ago to all the locally born, but not in the Malay States. There was excuse for the Malay attitude. Everywhere the Chinese and the Indians are inflexible in excluding the Malay from commerce. When the Kedah government once called for tenders for the erection of buildings and stipulated that a quarter of the labour force must be Malay, no Chinese or Indians would condone the breaking of their closed ring by tendering, though payment of ten per cent above the sum tendered was offered. When a Malay co-operative society tried to export its copra by a Chinese coastal steamer to Singapore, the first cargo was left on the jetty and the second was found on arrival to have mysteriously diminished. When the government gave loans to Perak fishermen to get them out of the clutch of the Chinese middleman, the Chinese manufacturers at Penang refused to sell the fisherman ice. Was it surprising that the Malay coming down with honours from Cambridge saw quite clearly that if he were edged out of the civil service also, then he was doomed to political as well as economic subordination in his own land? Why, he asked, should his country be ruled by aliens who came there for commercial advantage and had yet to exhibit political ability in the administration of their own homelands? The Malay knew, too, that before Whitehall precipitated its aborted Union, the Chinese, except for a few Straits-born with English ideas and education, were quite apathetic about Malayan politics, wanting neither government posts nor local citizenship. As a well-known member of the Chinese side of the civil service wrote at the time: "Popular demand for democratic representation there was none." The main interest thinking and responsible Chinese took in the stir created by the new policy, was as to its effect on trade. Would it accentuate racial hates and dislocate business?

Even before the Malay Rulers had been consulted, the Union was announced in the Commons as a *fait accompli*, and nothing excited more criticism than the method adopted to get the signatures of the Rulers to a treaty ceding to Great Britain full political power under the Foreign Jurisdiction Act of 1890. For Whitehall's emissary to the Rulers was entrusted with the dual functions of getting their signatures and of recognizing on behalf of the King the four who had succeeded to their thrones during the Japanese occupation, a joint errand that inevitably raised an outcry against *force majeur*. In most states, though not in Johore, a pretence was made of getting the consent of the Ruler-in-Council, but the Councils had been suspended by the British military authorities and legally did not exist. Where there were symptoms of recalcitrance Sir Harold MacMichael described how a civil servant in brigadier's uniform was put up to explain the new policy in Malay, "a method productive of excellent results". At best the explanations must have been vague, as the government had not yet elucidated its proposals. But the strangest features about these negotiations for a basis for Malaya's future democracy was the strict secrecy Sir Harold was enjoined to require from the Rulers, who by a British democracy were forbidden to divulge to their subjects transactions that must affect the future of the Malay race. There is no doubt that history, implacable in its final judgments, will condemn procedure neither in accordance with British ideals nor even with modern British practice in dealing with peoples far less civilized than the Malays.

All these points were raised in vigorous debates in both Houses, Viscount Elibank and Viscount Marchwood condemning the proposals in the Upper House and Captain Gammans, formerly of the Malayan Civil Service, leading the attack in the Commons. But perhaps the most notable protest was in a letter to *The Times* signed by seventeen retired officials who had held high appointments in Malaya. Among the signatories to that letter were a former Chief Justice and four gentlemen who had been Colonial Governors. Its final paragraph read:

"We deprecate the manner in which the people of the Straits Settlements and of the Malay States are being coerced by Orders-in-Council without regard to democratic principles, and finally we deprecate with all the emphasis at our command the issue of the preliminary Orders-in-Council, purporting to provide no more than a 'framework' for the immediate administration of Malaya, but in effect an instrument for the annexation of the Malay States."

The Government in the end left the matter of Singapore remaining a separate Colony for local decision, but over the Union of the Malay States it bowed to the storm. For encouraged by the attitude of their friends in Britain the Rulers refused to meet the new Governor officially; Malays refused to serve on the new Councils, and the Malay people wore mourning for a week. The upshot was that the British Government appointed a committee of representative Asiatics and British officials to explore the possibility of a *via media* that would placate Malay resentment. The advice of that committee was to change the Union into a Federation under a High Commissioner on the lines of the former federation of four states with the rights and status of the Rulers as representatives of their people left unimpaired. It recommended that the High Commissioner, like the Governor of a Colony, should have a small Executive Council of officials and unofficials to advise him. And the Malays in their anxiety to learn the methods of government asked that the example of Johore be followed by the creation of an Executive Council and a Malay Prime Minister for each state. The Committee's report was published for the information and views of the other races of Malaya and with few modifications was accepted in London and implemented in Malaya in 1948.

The new policy, while preserving the individuality of each state, aimed at a centralized uniform system of government, economical and safeguarding financial stability. There were therefore not only Legislative Councils for each state, but a Federal Legislative Council to consider and pass laws applicable to all the states. The federal legislature consisted of

81 members, including senior officials and 66 nominated unofficials, who represented racial minorities, trades unions, the tin and rubber industries and commerce. In 1955 the membership was increased to 98, of whom 46 were British officials (5) and unofficials nominated as before, and 52 were the elected representatives of territorial constituencies. The upshot of the 1955 election was that of the principal Asian races there were on the Council 50 Malays, 25 Chinese, 7 Indians and 2 Ceylonese, the Malays thus having a majority in a house where a Malay Speaker had already replaced the High Commissioner. The election was remarkable for the sweeping capture of all but one seat by a single party, the "Alliance" of the United Malay National Organization (U.M.N.O.) under Tengku Abdul-Rahman, a barrister son of a Kedah Sultan, and a Malayan Chinese Association (M.C.A.) under the titular headship of Dato' Sir Cheng Lok Tan of Malacca. It was U.M.N.O. that under Dato' Sir Onn bin Jaffar of Johore had defeated the Malayan Union, but growing conservatism in his outlook led Dato' Onn to found a new national party (*Parti Nègara*) in 1953, which advocating a gradual approach to self-government failed utterly to win the votes of the people or to provide any opposition in the new Council, although many Asians remained nervous about premature independence and fearful of an ultimate clash of interests between Malays and Chinese.

The preponderance of the "Alliance" in the Legislative Council gave its members preponderance in the Executive Council, which from 1948 had given the British High Commissioner a body of advisers consisting of important officials and prominent unofficial members of the legislature, six of whom held portfolios as ministers. Finally the sweeping victory of the "Alliance" with its unexpected accord of Malays and Chinese and its insistence that government of Asians by Asians for Asians might end the terrorism by Chinese Communists (which was costing the Federation one third of its revenue) led to the decision by Great Britain to promise Tengku Abdul-Rahman and his party independence within the British Commonwealth by 1957.

The most difficult problem for the Malay States was

that of citizenship, which is a necessary qualification for electoral rights and membership of any Council. From 1948 its acquisition became automatic for subjects of the Malay Rulers, for any person born in the Federation who habitually spoke Malay and followed Malay customs, for any British subject born in the Federation and resident there for fifteen years and for any British subject born in the Federation to a father born in Malaya or resident there for fifteen years. Citizenship could also be claimed (1) by applicants who had been born in the Federation and lived there for not less than eight out of the twelve years preceding the application, or (2) by immigrant foreigners who had lived in the Federation not less than fifteen out of twenty years preceding the application. In 1952 further legislation reduced the residential qualification to ten years, relaxed the language qualification, made all subjects of the Queen and the Malay Rulers automatically citizens of the Federation and also any applicant who, not being otherwise qualified, had served in the Armed Forces for two full years or four years of part-time. If for some approved purpose such as study, or if prior to the last decade, then continuous absence for five years would not disqualify. Qualifications for this citizenship was possessed by 40 per cent of the Chinese, but in 1954 only 150,000 Chinese had registered as voters against more than a million Malays, and there remains to be seen the political consequence of the gradual extension of citizenship to more and more of a people who with an ineradicable Chinese outlook will soon constitute the most energetic half of the population.

Not only changes in the constitution but the immigration of aliens and the welfare of Malays were the especial concern of a Conference of Rulers which meets five or six times a year. But the ultimate decision on immigration policy lay, in the case of dispute, with the unofficial members of the Federal Legislative Council.

CHAPTER XVI

AN INDEPENDENT MALAYA AND A SELF-GOVERNING SINGAPORE

The Federation of Malaya

On the 31st August, 1957, the nine Malay States along with the Settlements of Penang and Malacca became the independent Federation of Malaya. The treaty of 1948 was abrogated. The Queen ceased to exercise sovereignty over Penang and Malacca and to have jurisdiction over the Malay States, though the Federation remains within the Commonwealth and an agreement with Great Britain provides for the external defence of Malaya and mutual assistance, the request for assistance to be on the initiative of the Federation.

The government of the new independent Federation passed to a Parliament consisting of (1) a King or Yang di-pĕrtuan Agong, elected by and from the rulers every five years, (2) a Senate or Upper House of thirty-three members holding office for six years, two each to be elected by the legislative assemblies of the eleven states, and eleven nominated by the King and (3) a House of one hundred Representatives elected by the people every five years. A Prime Minister, appointed by the King, chooses a Cabinet, whose advice (or that of the Prime Minister) must be followed by His Majesty. If the Senate rejects a bill, it still becomes law, if after a lapse of twelve months the Lower House of Representatives so resolves. Agriculture and land are matters for the state governments; education and medical services for the Federal. But the Federal parliament can legislate on any subject to bring about uniformity, though to save face each state will separately adopt such legislation, such as (to take the most important example) a National Land Code. Judges are appointed by the Yang di-pĕrtuan Agong and appeal to the Privy Council is retained.

In the several states each ruler must accept the advice of

his Chief Minister (*Měntěri Běsar*) or Executive Council and, a Chief Minister is responsible to his State Legislative Assembly, of which he must be a member. Membership of these Assemblies is for four years. To give the states some say in finance, monetary grants to them are discussed by a National Council consisting of the Prime Minister, the Federal Finance Minister and the Chief Ministers of the various states.

Penang and Malacca have Governors appointed by the Yang di-pěrtuan Agong after consultation with the local governments.

Islam is the religion of the Federation with each ruler the head of that religion within his state. But all citizens are equal before the law and enjoy freedom to practise their own religion.

For the Malays a few special privileges are reserved. Acting on the advice of his Cabinet the Yang di-pěrtuan Agong must see that the Malays enjoy a reasonable proportion of posts in the public service (which is fixed now at four Malays to one of other races), of scholarships and of permits for the operation of any trade or business. When any land is reserved for Malays, an equal area must be set aside for other races. The official language is Malay and its study compulsory in all schools. English, also, will be taught in all schools and the study of Chinese and Tamil receives support.

Anyone who was a citizen of the Federation under the Agreement of 1948 remains a citizen of the independent Federation—one may become a citizen by birth, registration or naturalization—(1) citizens by birth are those born in one of the states (including Penang and Malacca) or born outside of a father who was a Malaya-born citizen or a government servant there at the time of the birth. If born abroad of a citizen father and kept abroad, the child yet becomes a citizen of Malaya if the birth is registered within a year at a Malayan consulate. Only citizens by birth are excused an oath of fealty to Malaya; (2) an adult (over eighteen) can become a citizen by registration if he or she has been born in the Federation, lived there for five out of the last seven years and intends to stay there: but after 31 August, 1958, an elementary knowledge of Malay was required. If not born in the Federation but resident there on the 31st August, 1957, the applicant's period of residence must have been eight years out of the last twelve; (3) to qualify for naturalization one must be over twenty-one, have served for three or four years in the armed forces or lived in the Federation for ten years out of the last twelve and have an adequate knowledge of Malay. The periods of residence required have been reduced from those of the 1948 Agreement in deference to Chinese protests.

The major problem of the new Malaya will be to secure continued co-operation between the Malays and Chinese, almost equal as they are in numbers. In his first address Malaya's King announced that "the economic needs of the country and independence demand that indigenous trading interests and especially Malay trading interests should be more closely associated with foreign interests in the accumulation of goods and services in the country. My government will encourage and assist Malays to have a greater share in commerce and industry." But will the Chinese change their traditional habits and co-operate towards the consummation of the government's aim? The Malays for their part have gone incredibly far to conciliate the stranger in their midst when the Sultan of Perak can sign a bill enabling one not a Malay to be chosen as Chief Minister of his State. The difficulty is that the pride of the Chinese and the religion of the Malay make intermarriage except in rare cases impossible. Already in 1945 the Society of Malay Students in England, a body far from bigoted, drew attention to the dominance of their religion and advocated a study of the possibility of "Indian and Chinese assimilation in Malay life and culture, the modern history of Europe and the Near East teaching the futility of forcing a fusion between races with conflicting ideas, allegiances and backgrounds". They added that Malay should be a compulsory subject for the entrance examination to Malaya's University. In the same year Sir Cheng Lock Tan, a leader of the Malaya-born Chinese, felt bound to insist that the government must foster the study of Chinese in schools to preserve Chinese culture. Even a separate Chinese University has been started in Singapore. And the point on which Chinese and Indian have been adamant is the preservation of their languages in the schools from fear lest their "national" cultures be destroyed.

Whatever the future may hold, "the Communist ferment in China, the nationalist ferment in Indonesia, the pride of an independent India circulated too strongly in the blood of the Malayans for Great Britain to halt the march of events and deny the demand for independence". It was during the seventy years of British protection that roads and railways and education replaced strong traditional jealousies between the states by a common sentiment of Malay nationalism. But it was the British attempt to foist on them the Malayan Union that first engendered a vehement patriotism and revealed to the Malay that he possessed political power. After that unhappy incident Whitehall endeavoured with unflagging zeal to urge peoples still indifferent to politics along the path to democracy, knowing that the Communist ideal can be countered only by another ideal, even if it is water compared with the heady wine of Marxism.

Communism existed in Malaya before the world war but was rendered innocuous by the banishment of undesirable aliens to their own country. After the Japanese occupation, disorganization of industry, inflation and shortage of food encouraged its spread, disciples finding a convenient channel for propaganda in a Pan-Malayan Federation of Trade Unions, which, indiscreetly fostered by the British, fomented strikes and violence. Heartened by these disturbances, a Communist Congress held at Delhi in March 1948 issued orders to Malaya's delegates to destroy the forces of law and order, disrupt communications, create panic by sabotage and seize an area to found a Communist republic. There were already bandits in the jungle delighted to get a directive that countenanced predatory activities. For to escape death at the hands of the Japanese there had fled into the forests of Malaya Chinese criminals released from the gaols in the hour of Britain's defeat and many able-bodied Chinese, some of them mere schoolboys who felt they were treading the path of Hollywood romance. Supplied with arms by the British they became guerillas fighting actually for China and looting Malay hamlets perforce for their food. When in their ignorance they thought China had won the war and that Malaya would become one of its provinces, sentimentality and disorganization combined to prevent these jungle allies from being made harmless. There were never more than 3000 to 5000 of them, and in four years that number was practically wiped out, to be replaced as it diminished by members of the Min Yuen, a Communist secret society (with some 15,000 members). During the same period, in spite of their exposure to a hidden foe, a slightly smaller number of troops, police and civilians of all races were killed or missing after encounters with terrorists, who slashed rubber-trees, intimidated tappers by torture and crucifixion, turned every planter's bungalow into a fort, derailed trains and ambushed and murdered passengers on the roads. Taken by surprise, the British had to train regiments in jungle warfare and recruit, train and equip local forces. The former competent police force with its reliable Chinese detectives was depleted by deaths and its loyal Asian cadre scattered. Measures for security were difficult to improvise and until a High Commissioner was murdered the gravity of the menace appeared to have been hardly appreciated sufficiently to ensure for local forces adequate arms and armoured cars. Originally it was hoped that the terrorists could easily be chased off the roads to be hunted down in the dense jungle. Even after eight years that was not accomplished, partly because a bandit could so easily exchange his gun for the deceptive disguise of a tapping knife. To combat this and deny food and supplies to the terrorist, Chinese squatters were collected into guarded settlements and the sale and transport of foodstuffs were controlled. An amnesty was offered in return for unconditional surrender. These measures led to many individuals giving themselves up, and military operations met with increasing success. But the hope that the independence of Malaya would see the end of terrorism was not immediately fulfilled. And when banditry ceased there still remained the political menace of Communism, the secular religion of China.

SINGAPORE

By April 1955 Singapore had a constitution that allotted twenty-five seats out of thirty-two in a Legislative Assembly

AN INDEPENDENT MALAYA 153

to elected members and out of an electorate of some three hundred thousand voters about half went to the polls at the first election. The embryo of a Cabinet existed in elected Ministers having charge of all departments except that for Defence and External Affairs. The Colony had advanced so far towards self-government that except for the powers of proroguing and dissolving the Legislative Assembly, the Governor when bound under the constitution to consult the Chief Minister had to act on his advice.

From this position development was rapid. On 3rd December 1959 the British Governor was replaced by a locally born Yang di-pĕrtuan Nĕgara, Enche' Yusuf bin Ishak, born in Taiping of Sumatran descent, a ruler appointed by the Queen after consultation with the Singapore government. His assent was required for laws, and he exercised the royal prerogative of mercy. Normally he would hold office for four years.

A United Kingdom Commissioner, appointed by the British Government, is chairman of a Council for Internal Security and of a committee on which the local government discusses its co-operation in matters connected with external defence and external relations, which remain the concern of Great Britain. The Commissioner will also assume the government of Singapore if at any time Great Britain should have to suspend the Constitution because the local government has acted contrary to it or in a manner threatening the British conduct of external affairs or defence.

The Legislative Assembly consists of fifty-one members all elected, with a Speaker of their own choice. There is a Council of Ministers chosen from members of the Legislative Assembly with its Prime Minister as chairman. Great Britain is no longer responsible for Singapore's internal government or for its commercial relations with foreign powers. The island, though not independent, is self-governing.

Citizenship is automatic for those born in Singapore, by registration for citizens of the British Commonwealth and those born in the Federation of Malaya who have lived on the island for two years, and for foreigners who have lived there for eight years, and finally by naturalization. All but the locally born must swear allegiance to the Queen and those born outside the Commonwealth must renounce their former nationality on oath. All but the locally born can be deprived of citizenship for disloyalty or disaffection and be deported.

As in the Federation the main problem is continuing co-operation between Malays and Chinese, so in Singapore a major problem is between those Chinese educated in their own language and those educated through the medium of English.

For financial, administrative and commercial reasons, it was natural for Singapore to want to be included in the Federation of Malaya, which however feared the preponderance of votes that a merger might give the Chinese at Federal elections. This difficulty was surmounted by the enlargement of the Federation to include Singapore, Sarawak and British North Borneo. Coming into being on 16th September, 1963, this far-flung area was termed Malaysia. Its creation excited the naval and military opposition of Indonesia, when British forces assisted Malaysia. In August 1965, Malaya expelled Singapore from Malaysia, the aims of its prime minister Lee Kuan Yew being irreconcilable with the Malay determination to retain for themselves certain privileges to counterbalance the commercial supremacy of the Chinese, who for their part admitted few but men of their own race into their businesses. Singapore became a republic but elected to remain a member of the British Commonwealth.

BIBLIOGRAPHY

JFMSM = *Journal of the Federated Malay States Museums.*
JIAEA = *Journal of the Indian Archipelago and Eastern Asia.*
JRASMB = *Journal of the Royal Asiatic Society, Malayan Branch.*
JRASSB = *Journal of the Royal Asiatic Society, Straits Branch.*
PMS = *Papers on Malay Subjects.*
All these periodicals contain valuable material for the study of Malaya and its inhabitants.

ARBERRY, A. J., and ROM LANDAU. *Islam Today.* London, 1943.
A chapter on Islam in Malaya is by R. O. Winstedt.
BARBOSA, DUARTE, *The Book of.* Hakluyt Society. 1918–21.
The author served the Portuguese Government in the East from 1500–17, and is one of the original authorities for the history of mediaeval Malacca.
BASTIN, J, *Essays on Indonesian & Malayan History.* Oxford, 1961.
BENNETT, LT.-GEN. H. GORDON. *Why Singapore Fell.* London, 1944.
A good account of the Japanese invasion of Malaya.
BORT, GOVERNOR BALTHASAR. "Report on Malacca, 1678." Tr. M. J. Bremner. *JRASMB*, Vol. V, Pt. 1, 1927.
Valuable for the history of Dutch rule in Malacca.
BOULGER, D. C. *The Life of Sir Stamford Raffles.* London, 1897.
A discursive life, full of material.
CHIN KEE ON. *Malaya Upside Down.* Singapore, 1946.
A first-hand account of Malaya under the Japanese.
CLIFFORD, SIR HUGH. *In Court and Kampong.* London.
—— *Studies in Brown Humanity.* London.
These tales give vivid accounts of Malay life just prior to British protection.
CLODD, H. P. *Malaya's First British Pioneer; the Life of Francis Light.* London, 1948.
CŒDÈS, G. "Le Royaume de Crivaya." *Bulletin de l'École Française d'Extrême-Orient.* Hanoi, XVIII, No. 6. 1918.
—— "Les Inscriptions Malaises de Crivijaya. *Ib.,* Vol. XXX. Nos. 1–2. 1930.
—— *Les États Hindouises d'Indochine et d'Indonésie.* Paris. 1948.
In 1918 Professor G. Cœdès first published his startling

discovery of the Malayo-Buddhist kingdom Sri Vijaya. His history is a masterly sketch of the hinduized kingdoms of South-East Asia including Malaya.

COUPLAND, SIR REGINALD. *Raffles, 1781-1826*. Oxford.
A general sketch of the life and work of the founder of Singapore.

COWAN, C. D. *Nineteenth-Century Malaya*. London, 1961.

D'ALBUQUERQUE'S "Commentaries". Tr. W. de G. Birch. Hakluyt Society. London, 1927. 3 Vols.
This work, by a natural son of the Portuguese conqueror of Malacca, is another of the sources for our knowledge of mediaeval Malacca.

DANVERS, F. C. *The Portuguese in India*. 2 Vols. London.
Inaccurate in detail, this work gives a good general idea of Portuguese rule in Asia.

DE MOUBRAY, G. A. DE C. *Matriarchy in the Malay Peninsula*. London, 1936.
A reliable study of the Minangkabau colonists of Negri Sembilan.

D'EREDIA, GODINHO. "Malacca, Meridional India and Cathay." Tr. by J. V. Mills. *JRASMB*, 1930. Vol. VIII.
Another Portuguese account of Malacca written after a century of Portuguese rule.

EMERSON, RUPERT. *Malaysia*. A Study in Direct and Indirect Rule (in Malaya and Netherlands India). New York, 1937.
A fully documented and expert work by a Harvard Professor, written with a bias against the old imperialism and so from an angle unfamiliar to most British students.

EVANS, I. H. N. *The Negritos of Malaya*, 1937.

FIRTH, RAYMOND. *Malay Fishermen: their Peasant Economy*. London, 1946.
An expert account of the fishermen of Kelantan.

FIRTH, ROSEMARY. *House-keeping among Malay Peasants*. London, 1943.
A detailed study of 1301 Kelantan folk, that should serve as a model for investigation into the economic structure of other Malay communities.

GIBSON, W. S. *See* G. Maxwell.

GIMLETTE, J. D. *A Dictionary of Malayan Medicine*. Oxford, 1939.
—— *Malay Poisons and Charm Cures*. London, 1929.
Exhaustive works on an interesting element in Malay culture.

HAHN, E. *Raffles of Singapore*. London, 1948.
   A lively account by a writer who has used Dutch sources.
HEINE-GELDERN, ROBERT. *Prehistoric Research in the Netherlands Indies*. South-East Asia Institute. New York, 1945.
   This summarizes the results of all prehistoric research in the Malayan region (including Malaya), and has a complete bibliography.
HURGRONJE, SNOUCK. *Mecca*.
   A reliable account of the Indonesian quarter and studies in Mecca.
JONES, S. W. *Public Administration in Malaya*. London, 1953.
KROM, N. J. *Hindu-Javaansche Geschiedenis*. The Hague, 1931.
LEUPE, P. A. "The Siege and Capture of Malacca from the Portuguese in 1640-1." (Extracts from the archives of the Netherlands East India Co.). Tr. by Mac Hacobian. *JRASMB*, Vol. XIV, Pt. 1. 1936.
   A first-hand account of the siege of Malacca in 1641.
LINEHAN, W. "A History of Pahang." *JRASMB*, Vol. XIV, Pt. 2. 1936.
   The only adequate history of an interesting State.
MAJUMDAR, R. C. *Suvarna-dvipa*. Political History. 1936.
—— ,, ,, Cultural History. 1938. Dacca.
   A scholarly account of Hindu influence in the Malay area.
—— *Hindu Colonies in the Far East*. Calcutta, 1944.
   A summary.
MAXWELL, SIR G. *In Malay Forests*.
   Charming tales of the jungle and the rural upcountry Malay.
—— *The Civil Defence of Malaya*.
   An authentic account of the Local Forces and Defence Services of Malaya at the time of the Japanese invasion, with chapters on the loyalty of its inhabitants and on the evacuation of Europeans.
MAXWELL and W. S. GIBSON. *Treaties and Engagements, Malay States and Borneo*. London, 1924.
   Indispensable for students of Malaya's political history.
MAXWELL, SIR WILLIAM E. "Law and Customs of the Malays with reference to tenure of land." *JRASSB*, Vol. XIII.
—— "Law relating to slavery among Malays." *JRASSB*

Vol. XII. Valuable articles describing conditions when British protection of the Malay States began.

McNair, Major F. *Perak and the Malays (Sarong and Kris).* London, 1878.
A good account of the early days of British protection.

Mills, L. A. "British Malaya, 1824-1867." *JRASMB*, Vol. III, Pt. 2. 1925.
A well-documented work on political and economic history, the civil service, the Chinese and piracy.

—— *British Rule in Eastern Asia.* London, 1942.
Indispensable for its account of all branches of modern British administration and endeavour in Malaya, based on a careful study of many official documents.

—— *Malaya. A Political and Economic Appraisal.* London, 1958.

Morrison, Ian. *Malayan Postscript.* London, 1942.
In spite of errors of fact and inference this is the best account of Malaya during the Japanese invasion.

Newbold, T. S. *Political and Statistical Account of British Settlements in the Straits of Malacca.* 2 Vols. London, 1939.
Valuable for its contemporary statistics and history.

Parkinson, C. N. *British Intervention in Malaya, 1867–1877.* Oxford, 1890.

Pires, Tomé. *The Suma Orientalis.* Tr. by A. Cortesao. 2 Vols. Hakluyt Society, 1944.
Written in Malacca, 1512-15. The most valuable of all Portuguese accounts of Malacca under the Malay Sultans. The MS. was lost until the translator discovered it in Paris in 1937.

Purcell, Victor. (1) *Malaya, Outline of a Colony.* T. Nelson and Sons Ltd. London, 1946
A readable and well-informed outline.

—— (2) *The Chinese in Malaya.* Oxford, 1948.
An expert account.

Rigby, J. *Law, Pt. II. The Ninety-Nine Laws of Perak. PMS*, 1908.
The eighteenth-century laws of Perak with translation.

Rose, Major Angus. *Who Dies Fighting.* London, 1944.
An account of what the author saw of the fighting during the Japanese invasion, with a lively criticism of British tactics.

Sastri, K. A. N., "Sri Vijaya". *Bulletin de l'École Française d'Extrême-Orient.* Hanoi. Tome XL, fasc. 2 (1940-1).
Contains full bibliography.

BIBLIOGRAPHY

SCHEBESTA, P. *Among the Forest-Dwarfs of Malaya.* London, 1939.
> A recent book on Malaya's aborigines by a trained observer: defaced by absurd exaggerations about the jungle.

SCHURHAMMER, REV. G., S.J. *St. Francis Xavier.* Tr. by F. J. Eble. London, 1928.

SHAW, G. E. Malay Industries. Pt. 3, "Rice Planting". *PMS*, 1911.
> A summary of the existing knowledge.

SKEAT, W. W. *Malay Magic.* London, 1900.
> A mine of information on Malay beliefs and magical practices, with an appendix of invocations in Malay.

—— and C. O. BLAGDEN. *Pagan Races of the Malay Peninsula.* 2 Vols. London, 1906.
> A summary of all information at the date of publication, with an invaluable comparative vocabulary of the languages.

STEWART, F. A. *The Life of St. Francis Xavier.* London, 1917.

SWETTENHAM, SIR FRANK. *British Malaya.* London.
> The earlier chapters are quite obsolete. The chapters on the author's own time are valuable, though that time is not seen in perspective but with contemporary eyes. The account of the Pangkor treaty is incomplete.

—— *Malay Sketches.* London.
—— *The Real Malay.* London.
> These stories of men and events in the early dates of British protection have vivid reality and show a deep knowledge of the Malay of the period.

TAYLOR, E. N. "Customary Law of Rembau." *JRASMB*, Vol. VII, 1929.
—— "Malay Family Law." *JRASMB*, Vol. XV, 1937.
—— "Mohammedan Divorce" by Khula.
—— "Inheritance in Negri Sembilan." *JRASMB*, Vol. XXI, 1948.
> Four of the best articles on Malay law.

WHEATLEY, P. *The Golden Khersonese.* Oxford, 1961.

WILKINSON, R. J. *Life and Customs.* Pt. 1. "The Incidents of Malay Life." *PMS*.
—— "Law." Pt. 1. Introductory Sketch. *PMS*. Kuala Lumpur. 1908.

Mr. Wilkinson was the author of a large Malay-English Dictionary and wrote many pamphlets that inspired later writers. The two pamphlets here cited have not yet been superseded.

WINSTEDT, R. O. *The Malays: a Cultural History.* London, 1962.

—— "A History of Malaya." Singapore, 1962.

—— "A History of Malay Literature." *JRASMB*, Vol. XVII, Pt. 3. 1940. Reprinted 1962.

—— *Malay Proverbs.* London, 1950.

—— *Malaya.* Editor of. London, 1923. (Chapter XIV has been superseded by the editor's later work, and Chapter XV is obsolete.)

—— *The Malay Magician.* London, 1961.

See Arberry, A.J.

All these books have very full bibliographies.

WRIGHT A. and REID, T. H. *The Malay Peninsula.* London, 1912.
A readable work on modern Malaya with chapters based on original research.

WURTZBURG, C. E. *Raffles of the Eastern Seas.* London, 1954.
The latest and fullest biography.

INDEX

Aborigines, 7, 10, 13-4, 103, 112
Acheh, 30, 32, 43-4, 46, 48-9, 62, 76, 118
Agriculture, 112-7
Alexander the Great, 37-8
Arabs, 16, 21, 30, 37-8, 41, 104, 118
Australo-Melanesoids, 7, 13, 14

British in Malaya, 22, 76; administration, 78-95; law, 96-102; social services, 124-34
Buddhism, 24-6, 28-30, 103, 118
Bugis (from Celebes), 10, 16, 52, 59, 60, 62-3, 76, 106

Census (1947), 18, 20-2
Chinese, 16, 18-20, 25, 30, 33-5, 41, 52-3, 60-4, 69, 70, 73, 76, 79, 81-2, 85, 88-90, 92, 94, 104, 106-8, 114-5, 117, 119, 121-2, 126, 129, 130, 132-4, 139, 140, 142-4, 149-50
Chola invasion, 30
Citizenship, Malayan, 147, 149-50
Coconuts, 114-5
Commerce, 25, 31, 35-6, 47, 52, 60, 103-111
Communism, 151-2

Decentralization, 91-3
Dutch, the, 7, 47-52, 55-60, 62, 76, 96, 105-7, 116, 118, 125, 129

East India Company, 22, 53, 78-82, 97
Education, 45, 130-4
Eurasians, 22, 52, 82

Fauna, 11
Federated Malay States, 88-91

Federation of Malaya, 145, 148-52; citizenship in, 147
Finance, public, 109-11
Fishing, 120-3
Flora, 9

Gold, 119

Health, public, 127-30
Hinduism, 7, 24-31, 99-101, 103, 128, 131
Husain, Sultan, 77

Immigration, 18, 20-2, 60, 141-3, 147
Indians, 20-1, 34-8, 40-1, 50, 52, 103-6, 113, 126-7
Industries, 112-23
Iron, 120
Islam, 17, 19, 37-9, 46, 130-1

Jakun, 13-4
Jambi (Melayu), 16, 30
Japanese, 120, 135-9
Java (and Javanese), 7, 31, 32, 34-6, 42-3, 50, 56, 104, 112-4, 126, 130
Johore, 14, 43-4, 48-9, 58-9, 61-4, 71-2, 76, 90, 92-4, 100, 103, 115

Kedah, 10, 13, 15, 18, 24, 30, 32, 34, 36, 48, 50-5, 61, 75, 90, 92, 94, 96, 100, 104-5, 110, 112-3, 117-8, 135, 143
Kelantan, 10-1, 13, 15-6, 18, 28-31, 75, 90, 94, 111, 113-4, 118, 122, 135

INDEX

Labour, 124–7
Langkasuka, 18, 28, 30, 33, 113
Law, 96–102
Light, Francis, 53–5, 78, 125
Literature, Malay, 21, 37–9, 130–1

Majapahit v. Java, 7–8, 31, 32–5
Malacca, under Malay rule, 32–9; under Portuguese, 40–9; under Dutch, 47–52; under British, 55–7, 79, 80; ceded by Holland, 88; independence of, 134
Malay administration, 82–7; education, 130–1; kingship, 85; medicine, 127–9; industries, 112–23; race, 14–7; religions: Hindu, 25–31, 99–101, 103, 128; Islamic, 17, 19, 37–9, 46, 130–1; States, 62–77; trade, 103–9
Malaya, the name, 8–9; physical features, 9–12; Federation of, 145–7; independent, 148–52
Malayan Union, 95, 140–5
Malaysia, 154
Meru, Mount, 27, 85
Minangkabaus, 10, 16, 27, 43, 51, 62, 76, 82–5, 115, 125
Mining, 118–20

Naning, 16, 56–7, 115
Negri Sembiean, 26–7, 35, 62–3, 70–2, 77, 82–5, 118

Opium, Indian, 55

Pahang, 10, 15, 30–1, 35, 43–4, 48, 63, 72–5, 88, 100, 118–20
Pasai, 32, 34, 36, 38

Penang, 11, 53–5, 59, 61, 78–9 97, 107, 119, 141
Pepper, 117
Perak, 27, 29, 35, 43–4, 50, 54, 62–3, 65–9, 85, 88–9, 100–1, 103, 118, 140
Portuguese, 7, 40–51, 76, 96, 114, 117, 118
Proto-Malays, 14

Races, of Malaya, 7, 13–23
Raffles (Sir) Thomas Stamford, 57–61, 80–1, 129
Rice-planting, 112–4
Rubber, 115–7

Sakai (Senoi), 13
Selangor, 32, 35, 62–5, 70
Siam, 21, 27, 32, 54–5, 108
Singapore, 8, 29, 57–61, 80, 95, 107–9, 134, 141, 152–4
Slavery, 124–6
Sri Vijaya, 7, 18, 29–31, 33–5, 39, 104
Straits Settlements, 78–94

Tin, 118–9
Trade, 103; royal, 105; free, 107–9

Unfederated Malay States, 92–5

Vijaya, Sri v. Sri Vijaya

Xavier, St. Francis, 44–5

Zabag, 30

For Product Safety Concerns and Information please contact our EU
representative GPSR@taylorandfrancis.com
Taylor & Francis Verlag GmbH, Kaufingerstraße 24, 80331 München, Germany

www.ingramcontent.com/pod-product-compliance
Lightning Source LLC
Chambersburg PA
CBHW061451300426
44114CB00014B/1925